STONEWALL INN EDITIONS
Keith Kahla, General Editor
Mikel Wadewitz, Associate Editor

D1246187

Buddies by Ethan Mordden
Joseph and the Old Man
  by Christopher Davis
Blackbird by Larry Duplechan
Gay Priest by Malcolm Boyd
One Last Waltz by Ethan Mordden
Gay Spirit by Mark Thompson, ed.
God of Ecstasy by Arthur Evans
Valley of the Shadow
  by Christopher Davis
Love Alone by Paul Monette
The Boys and Their Baby
  by Larry Wolff
On Being Gay by Brian McNaught
Living the Spirit by Will Roscoe, ed.
Everybody Loves You
  by Ethan Mordden
Untold Decades by Robert Patrick
Gay & Lesbian Poetry in Our Time
  by Carl Morse
  and Joan Larkin, eds.
Tangled Up in Blue
  by Larry Duplechan
How to Go to the Movies
  by Quentin Crisp
The Body and Its Dangers and Other
  Stories by Allen Barnett
Dancing on Tisha B'Av
  by Lev Raphael
Arena of Masculinity
  by Brian Pronger
Boys Like Us by Peter McGehee
Don't Be Afraid Anymore
  by Reverend Troy D. Perry
  with Thomas L. P. Swicegood
The Death of Donna-May Dean
  by Joey Manley
Sudden Strangers by Aaron Fricke
  and Walter Fricke
Latin Moon in Manhattan
  by Jaime Manrique
On Ships at Sea by Madelyn Arnold
The Dream Life by Bo Huston

Sweetheart by Peter McGehee
Show Me the Way to Go Home
  by Simmons Jones
Winter Eyes by Lev Raphael
Boys on the Rock by John Fox
End of the Empire by Denise Ohio
Tom of Finland
  by F. Valentine Hooven III
Reports from the Holocaust,
  revised edition by Larry Kramer
Created Equal by Michael Nava
  and Robert Dawidoff
Gay Issues in the Workplace
  by Brian McNaught
Sportsdykes by Susan Fox Rogers, ed.
Sacred Lips of the Bronx
  by Douglas Sadownick
The Violet Quill Reader
  by David Bergman, ed.
West of Yesterday, East of Summer
  by Paul Monette
I've a Feeling We're Not in Kansas
  Anymore by Ethan Mordden
Another Mother by Ruthann Robson
Pawn to Queen Four by Lars Eighner
Coming Home to America
  by Torie Osborn
Close Calls by Susan Fox Rogers, ed.
How Long Has This Been Going On?
  by Ethan Mordden
My Worst Date by David Leddick
Girljock: The Book by Roxxie, ed.
The Necessary Hunger
  by Nina Revoyr
Call Me by P-P Hartnett
My Father's Scar by Michael Cart
Getting Off Clean
  by Timothy Murphy
Mongrel by Justin Chin
Now That I'm Out, What Do I Do?
  by Brian McNaught
Some Men Are Lookers
  by Ethan Mordden

Also by Justin Chin

Bite Hard

MONGREL

Essays, Diatribes, and Pranks

MONGREL

ESSAYS, DIATRIBES, AND PRANKS

Justin Chin

St. Martin's Press ☎ New York

MONGREL: ESSAYS, DIATRIBES, AND PRANKS.
Copyright © 1999 by Justin Chin. All rights reserved. Printed in the
United States of America. No part of this book may be used or reproduced
in any manner whatsoever without written permission except in the case of
brief quotations embodied in critical articles or reviews. For information,
address St. Martin's Press, 175 Fifth Avenue, New York, NY 10010.

Design by: JAMES SINCLAIR

Library of Congrss Cataloging-in-Publication Data

Chin, Justin.
    Mongrel : essays, diatribes, and pranks / Justin Chin. — 1st
Stonewall Inn ed.
        p.   cm.
    ISBN 0-312-19513-3
    1. Chin, Justin.   2. Authors, American—20th century—Biography.
3. Asian Americans—California—San Francisco—Social life and
customs.   4. Gay men—United States—Biography.   5. Asian
American gays—Biography.   I. Title.
PS3553.H48973Z47   1998
818'.5409—dc21
[B]   98-37185
                                                                      CIP

First Stonewall Inn Edition: January 1999

10 9 8 7 6 5 4 3 2 1

To Lisa & to Dave

CONTENTS

CHAIN LETTER

Dear Friend of Literature:

Enclosed is a very good book. In fact, it is more than supergood. It is fucking brilliant. Please take the time out to read the book and recommend it to eight others. If you do not wish to read the book or find that you cannot finish it for whatever reason (book too long, too verbose, failing eyesight, leprosy, etc.), please give the book to someone else who will appreciate it and also recommend it to eight others. PLEASE DO NOT IGNORE THIS LETTER. Aloysious Wong, of Hoboken, heeded it and now his first novel, I Don't Know What Race I Am (I'm So Confused), *is currently being shopped around at A MAJOR NEW YORK PUBLISHER with film rights in the works. On the other hand, Geri-Ann Shimizu, of Honolulu, chose to ignore this letter and, to date, her only publishing credit is her poem "Flip Flops at Sandy Beach," published in the spring 1998 issue of* Bamboo Canyon. *It was on the left side of a Juli-Anna Shibata Lee-Nelson poem and so only four people read it. The fifth* reader, Geri-Ann's babe, Scott Nishimoto-Newman, only made it halfway through because he couldn't understand it. Catherina Sung, of White Christmas Valley Canyon, received this chain and chose to ignore it and her second book, Memories of Sewing and Cooking with My Mother, went unnoticed. She later remembered the chain and passed it on and her third book, A Sewing and Cooking Girlhood, is currently #11 at the Waimea Barnes and Noble bestest-seller list. Her neighbor also carried on the chain and her dog had beautiful puppies. M Prince, of Twenty Nine Palms, California, broke the chain and he developed several canker sores while reading the new John Grisham best-seller and could not enjoy the book. You get the picture. Please do not break the chain. We want only good things to happen to you. THIS IS NOT A JOKE. Do it now and good things will befall you.

Thank you.

MONSTER

The first gay people I knew were not called gay at all. They were the drama queens at school, Nellie boys who lived for the annual music and drama night where they would take over an empty classroom to pile on their makeup, stagger in their heels, and shimmy up tight dresses fit for the trashiest lounge singers in Bras Basah Road. These were the boys destined for the infamous Bugis Street, but that was before the government tore the street down and rebuilt it to tourist efficiency, complete with government-approved drag queens. The queens were called fairies, homos, a-quas, ba-pok, derogatory names for their effeminacy. But the queens wore these epithets like general's epaulets, or more like Joan Collins–inspired shoulder pads. On that one night, they sashayed across the basketball court to the auditorium in their female drag, ignoring the most hostile name-calling, flirting with the milder name-calling, and simply wallowing in all the attention.

Out of drag, in their regular school life, they hung together, designed dresses in the margins of their textbooks, gave each other girl names, and flirted shamelessly with the boys on the swim team. They joined the drama club, where they vied for the female roles onstage, giving them an excuse to get into drag and be applauded for it for one brief moment one night of the year. They dreamed of having a sex change, owning a boutique, dating the captain of the swim team, and being a fashion designer or model or air stewardess, not necessarily in that order.

The boys at school were either vastly entertained by the queens or were grossed out and quite violent toward them. I was of the former, but then, I had to be. I knew I liked boys, and the stigma of being associated with the queens who were so resoundingly ribbed and teased and tormented made me nestle quite firmly in my comfy closet: I was on the swim team, I participated in sports—something the queens never dreamed of doing. I outran and outswam many of my classmates. Still, the closet door was at least somewhat ajar. I had my campy side: I could do a great Madonna circa "Like A Virgin" impersonation, but somehow, the butchness dulled any hostility toward it, and I was accepted by the "problem kids," the ones who sat in the back of the class, didn't pay attention, skipped school, and generally raised hell; our teachers predicted that we were destined to all kinds of failure and a future as worthless wage slaves.

I knew, or rather, discovered to my horror quite early on that I wasn't entirely heterosexual. In Primary Six (sixth grade), the hormones started to rage through my baby-fat body, pubic hairs started to peek out of my crotch and armpits, my voice started to change, and I was made aware that I had a penis. My brother complained to my mother that I was still running around the house without my pajama bottoms on. The first pangs of homosexuality struck while reading a Buck Rogers book. I had strange feelings deep in my gut when the author described Buck's torso. The story involved alien women in primary colors who kidnap Buck and try to get impregnated with his seed so that they can propagate their race.

Those feelings arose again when Harrison Ford, as dashing space bounty hunter Han Solo, was on the cover of *GQ* magazine. This time I went one step further and I hid in the bathroom and kissed the magazine's glossy cover. Then it surfaced again. Now it was *Magnum PI*, Friday nights at 9:30 P.M.

These feelings and preoccupations terrified me. I grew up in a decidedly Christian household. The year before, my guardian, who was an elder at the church, had taken in Betty, the church secretary, who was possessed by the devil. Betty needed a place to stay while the church elders prayed over her, and my aunt opened the house to her. The weeks that Betty stayed were filled with her screaming and the strange babble of her and the elders speaking in tongues, a verbal tussle between God and the devil. To quell our fears, my aunt decided that we should have Bible study and prayer meetings every night. We rid the house of anything that might have harbored the devil: images of dragons, phoenixes, tikis, and any trinket or drawing that looked scary, Gothic, ghostly, or primitive. We prayed a lot and we were constantly aware of the devil lurking in every corner.

Still, I couldn't quell these feelings inside of me. I wanted so much to see another penis: my father's, uncle's, celebrities' in a magazine, anyone's. I scanned through my father's medical textbooks that he stored under my brother's bed for pictures of penises, and I found them in all their diseased glory: bulbous members plagued with syphilis, gonorrhea, and other sores and boils. I read Dr. David R. Reuben's *Everything You Wanted to Know About Sex, But Were Afraid to Ask*, and was titillated by the sexual details described in the book. I looked in the dictionary to see what I would find in the words *penis*, *homosexual*, and *intercourse*. I figured out how to masturbate one day when I was trying to put on a makeshift condom, and I took to masturbation with a passion. I bought the "Best Body Poll" issue of *Tiger Beat* and took great guilt and secret delight in it. (Scott Baio won best body, Gregory "Gonzo Gates" Harrison got a paltry twelfth place.) I rode around on my bike looking for men without their shirts on.

One day, on my way to school, this man, an ugly-looking fucker, sat beside me on the school bus. Suddenly, he placed his hand on my crotch and covered his act with my school bag. I was shocked, frightened, and excited at the same time. At my stop, I got off the bus and he followed me. He said to follow him and that we could go to the rest room to "play." It never occurred to me to say no. In the toilet stall, he started sucking my nipples, he sucked my dick. I had no idea what to do. He pushed my mouth to his ugly cold nipple but I didn't really know what was expected of me. He then tried to force me to suck his dick. This I knew was what was expected of me and when he forced his dick into my mouth, I gagged so hard I started vomiting. Undaunted, he tried to fuck me in the ass. By this time, I was scared and close to the verge of tears, and, in fact, I think I was crying. Thankfully, he came and he left. I spent a good deal of time locked in the stall, trying to clean up, crying and praying to God for forgiveness.

All this should have soured me somewhat on men's penises, but it only made me more confused and needful. One day, something accidental happened that would change my life. I discovered that at a urinal, I could actually see someone's penis. I was ecstatic and fearful, but I wanted more. One day, at a local shopping mall, as I was trying to sneak a peek at penises, a man at the urinal actually turned to me and started playing with himself. The whole world of rest room sex opened itself up to me. I was thirteen years old.

Soon, I was spending a great deal of time hanging out in shopping malls and cruising the rest rooms for sexual encounters. My rest-room exploits started to be a great burden on my mind. My homosexual longings developed the strongest in the same year as my confirmation and baptism, a fabulous, *très* dramatic Brethren baptism where I was dipped into the the chlorinated waters of the church baptismal pit and pulled out free from sin, washed with the holy spirit. I was wracked with a lot of guilt, and the better part of the year was spent making deals with God, asking God for a sign, ignoring and rationalizing everything I perceived to be a sign, praying for forgiveness, and being obsessed with raging hormones and a seemingly endless supply of dicks. I believed that it was all part of a test by God to see if I were sinning. I was. I believed I was destined for hell. I believed in the Rapture, in the Book of Revelation, a story that had been read to me when I was a mere child and every time there was a thunderstorm, my heart would collapse and I would fear the Rapture, that the good Christ-fearing folk would be snatched up from the earth and the rest of the sinners would be left to fight the end of the millennium against the Antichrist.

I fucked a lot in those teenage days. At some point, I very distinctly remember that I had lost count of the number of men that I had tricked with. I fucked flight attendants on layovers (Quantas seemed to have the highest number of fags), sailors, potbellied tourists, professors, bankers, businessmen, all strangers and very few repeats. Some tried to stay in touch; some fell hopelessly in love at first fuck and wanted to marry me. I didn't know any better. I wanted more. I had no idea what I wanted. And at some point, and I don't particularly remember when, I stopped praying for forgiveness.

I'm also not sure exactly where and when I got the language for who and what I am. I don't remember how I learned the words gay, homo (sexual), fag, queen, etc. I just seemed to have picked them up and understood what they meant.

With the closet door ajar, and with my ear to the crack, I watched and heard what people said and how they reacted to gay life. Some were pleasant and tolerant, others were horrified and vicious. The names called and used to describe *that life* were used lovingly and violently at the same time. It didn't matter what I was called, I realized—*sticks and stones* . . . as they say—but who I was to be. And from the periphery of that closet, I learned to piece together who I was as a little queer.

The first person that I knew who publicly admitted to being gay was Gary, whom I met through a common friend, someone I had picked up but never ended up having sex with. I was seventeen, in junior college, on the slippery pipeline to my "A" level examinations, which would determine which college I could attend and which major I could take. I was failing every subject miserably. (E for biology, O for chemistry and physics, F for math, though I got an A for my English general paper.) Gary 'fessed up to being gay during the compulsory National Military Service. He declared himself "effeminate homosexual" which got him a desk job, a pass to leave every evening, and visits to the staff psychiatrist who suggested Gary play more sports with his father. At a time when I was coming to the realization that freedoms were fast disappearing— my wild teenage years were slipping into adult responsibilities, and at a time when everywhere we looked, it seemed that the government had its grip on everything: a group of Catholic missionaries and a local theater group had just been arrested for allegedly spreading communistic thoughts; magazines such as the *Asian Wall Street Journal* and *Newsweek* were restricted under a newly adopted law that limited the print run of magazines that criticized the Singaporean government—I thought that Gary's bold declaration was such a courageous act. Gloria Gaynor singing "I Am What I Am" paled in comparison.

Gary was by no stretch of the imagination an a-qua. He wanted to be a fashion designer; he was involved in the local theater scene and he designed many a fabulous costume. Today, he's made a name for himself as one of Singapore's up-and-coming young designers. I always looked at him as sort of a hero, as someone who lived as he wanted to and made everyone around him accept it or deal with it. He had no qualms about being a flaming queen in public. Once, we were out together and I was so incredibly embarrassed when he started spinning and dancing in the middle of a shopping center simply because the Bananarama tunes wafting out of a shop moved him so. He had balls, that boy did.

Soon, I discovered the gay underbelly of Singapore. I started going to gay bars and discotheques. I had gay friends. I fell in love with men who broke my teenage heart. I met a Swedish psychologist who became my first boyfriend. (He was rather abusive, wholly narcissistic, unrelentingly colonial, and it ended miserably.

But God, he was so damn good-looking.) I started being even more comfortable with my homosexuality, I stopped being wracked with guilt and plunged headfirst into my homosexuality, dating, having gay friends, having sex without guilt. I was still struggling with that closet, with being found out by my family, but in school, I was the out fag. I was so out, that in retrospect, I am amazed that I wasn't harassed at all. I believe my impunity from the really horrid harassment other queens faced had to do with my intersecting butch and queer appearances. My friends, straight girls and really cool straight guys, protected me a lot, too. To them, my queerness was incidental to my personality. They accepted me because they knew me first as this guy who hated and liked the same things and the same people they did. Knowing that, the knowledge that I was a fag didn't change their opinions of me or our friendship.

I left home to come to the United States when I was eighteen. I decided that I really didn't need to tell my family about my sexual orientation. Sure, they had their suspicions, and even voiced them, but I had always somehow managed to change the subject much to the relief of us all.

But as the trickledown theory would have it, my outness in one arena soon seeped into the other. My brother and my childhood friends became friends with my friends from junior college. Soon, more people than I bargained for *knew*. They were very subtle and careful about bringing up the subject to me, but by this point, I wasn't particularly bothered by it anymore. Out of the blue, I got a nice supportive and very subtle note from my brother. My best childhood friend was quite miffed that I had never seen fit to tell him sooner.

I don't have any regrets about how I learned how to be gay. Perhaps I harbor some romantic notions about the traditional coming out. Perhaps how I came out is not what we wish for our younger generations; that it consisted of nothing but severe and superficial sexual experiences, all done without that hesitant first crush, the awkward horseplay behind the barn, and all that other really affirming, charming, and homo-positive things that you might in coming-out books published by Alyson Books and Gay Sunshine Press in the early eighties.

I guess I never *really* came out in any sense of that word, whatever that means. After coming to terms with my desires, I simply tried to live my life the best way I knew how, and as much and as unapologetically as I knew how. With that, people came to their own realizations that I was queer. Telling someone that I am gay really holds no appeal to me. It doesn't mean a thing. I would rather folks see that I live and love in the same way and in the same breath as they do, but in a queer way and in my queer way. And if they find a monster in that, I'll know that it is a monster of grace and beauty.

SAVED

They have names like "Love In Action," "Where Grace Abounds," "Worthy Creations," "Restoration Inc.," "Freedom at Last," and "Free!" These gung ho New Age–sounding names are, in fact, part of a web of Christian ministries attempting to lead gays and lesbians out of "the life."

These, and many others with equally winsome names, are under the wing of Exodus International, described in their literature as "a worldwide coalition of Christian ministries dedicated to helping men and women who struggle with homosexuality to find change from their broken sexual orientation and sinful sexual behaviors through the transforming power of Jesus Christ."

Based in San Rafael, California, Exodus International governs more than 250 drop-in groups and three live-in residential programs in San Rafael, Memphis, and Wichita. Exodus International also makes good on its name: It has live-in programs in Manila and London as well as counseling programs in Australia, Canada, and Singapore.

Exodus refers people who contact them to ministries in their area. It also runs a mail-order service that sells books, pamphlets, audiotapes, and videos that deal with a full buffet of homo-esque subjects: AIDS, teenage crushes, promiscuity, sexual abuse, transvestitism, cross-dressing, pedophilia, how to respond to gay Christians, and being married to a gay or "ex-gay."

Any Christian ministry that wants to be an Exodus referral organization can simply apply to the organization. The ministry will be screened for its commitment to the cause, its abilities, and the resources it offers. But Exodus does have a rather hands-off approach once it accepts a ministry. Hence, prospective ex-gays may find different degrees of tenacity, evangelism, fanaticism, or misguidance.

Perhaps it is fitting that Exodus International is based in the San Francisco Bay Area, given the area's reputation as the nation's gay mecca. A very cheery woman answers the phone when I call, and she readily gives me the information I ask for. In the Bay Area, there are four places that can help, she tells me: New Hope Ministries/Church of the Open Door in San Rafael; Transformed Image in San Jose; New Ministries in San Leandro; and Martin Wong, a psychologist who practices in San Francisco and Fremont. She gives me their phone numbers and the name of the person to contact. "Good luck with your journey," she tells me before I hang up.

"The problem we have is with people of the same sex and not of the opposite sex. We need to affirm our masculine selves and we need same-sex affirmation that is nonsexual," Frank Worthen pronounces, and the gathered group nod their heads like trained seals.

When Frank Worthen speaks, ex-gays prick up their ears. Worthen is often called the Father of Ex-Gay Ministries. He is the author of a number of books, the most famous being *Stepping Out of Homosexuality*, which New Hope Ministries uses like a Bible, or at least a twelve-step handbook.

Worthen is head honcho of New Hope Ministries, a part of the Church of the Open Door. Worthen is one of the early pioneers of the ex-gay movement. He founded Love In Action in 1973 and ran it till 1991. He left to go to Manila to start a mission there; Love In Action moved to Memphis.

But he's back with New Hope and runs a live-in program at a mid-size duplex apartment complex in the quaint and leafy suburb of San Rafael. The live-in program is a big deal. It is terribly competitive and the push for someone to enroll begins very early on. I'm constantly told that it's my best bet for curing my homosexuality and that it takes *real commitment* to be in the live-in program. Of course, the unsaid inference of that piece of information is that if I don't want to be in the live-in, I'm simply not taking my program too seriously and I'm doomed to a life of homosexual vices and the "deep devastation" (i.e., suicide, alcoholism, AIDS, according to their literature) sowed in the lives of those who are involved in homosexuality.

When I first contact the Church of the Open Door, Don, who was answering the hot line that day, tells me about the program and how it is run. Every year, people from all over the United States and abroad apply to be accepted into the one-year program which begins every New Year's Eve. The program accepts about ten people each year, their applications and three reference letters having been scrutinized by the ministry for things like "spiritual maturity" and commitment to the program. The program costs

$600 a month and the participants live in the apartment with a roommate for the year. The participants go to work in the morning but are expected to have their nights and weekends free for meetings, Bible studies, and socials.

I tell him that I can't simply apply for the program, as I need to work and go to college and I have bills to pay. "Many people put college and careers on hold for a year because this is so necessary," he counters.

Once in the program, the participants are taught to be "better stewards of time." For the first three months, each participant is not allowed to be alone, nor go anywhere alone outside of work. A group of two or three is required, and eventually, when one becomes "a better steward of time," he or she is allowed more private time. Presumably if a gay man is left to himself, he'll inevitably be thinking of well-oiled beefcake while masturbating in the bathroom.

Even while at work, the program's participants aren't left all that much alone either: Many of the participants work for the church or are employed in menial office work by a company. At my first meeting, a man tells me how a former program member has just joined the staff of the insurance company he works at. "That makes ten of us working for them, or have worked for them," he says. "They're great, there's so many of us there and they understand when we need time off."

Every Sunday, the entire house goes to the Church of the Open Door together. Every year, the members of the house are introduced to the church, which is attended by many ex-gays and ex–program members. Members of the church receive little bookmarks with the program participants' short biographies so that the church member can pray for them through the year. This year, the house's participants have come from Manila, Sweden, and from around America. The Swede had to leave a month ago because his visa ran out and could not be renewed.

But since I'm not going to try for the live-in program, there is the drop-in support group, Don says. And the support group is "a good thing because whatever you've gone through, everyone there has heard it before." So, on a muggy Friday night, six of us are sitting in New Hope's rec room bonding in our struggle with "the life."

This was my second meeting at New Hope, but my first with Worthen. The first time I attended a meeting, Worthen was out of town at Exodus's annual conference.

If anyone is to be accused of stereotypically, or even archetypically, gay behavior, it would be this group gathered on this Friday night in a pastel, sofa-laden rec room that sports an unused bar and a bit of forced butchness: a weight-training station. We have the limp-wristed queen, the mustached clone, the chubby, the drama queen with goatee, the army dude, the flight attendant.

With their mentor away, the meeting was low-key and the other participants and I took turns reading aloud from Worthen's book. The men offered encouragements ("God is patient and always there when you need him." "I was weeding when I asked God to help me and in my prayer I pulled out a chunk of weeds, roots and all, and I realized that that was the way I had to do it, roots and all."), told of how they fed their homosexual urges (Damon: "I would buy *Teen Beat* and drool over David Cassidy."; Don: "Ah, [strange lip-smacking noise] Vincent Van Patten."), and discussed how Worthen's writing had so succinctly applied to their lives and just what great guys he and his wife, Anita, are.

But Worthen is back at the roost, and the group is sharing stories with Vern, a first-timer.

Jim: molested by his grandfather for fourteen years; left college; became a flight attendant and fell into a "hell of perversion," living fast and promiscuous; entered a relationship with a man for seven years; broke up, went into a severe depression; was hospitalized, medicated, and went through shock treatments, and then applied to the live-in program.

Ralph: lived a double life going to church and adult bookstores with the same fanaticism; was suicidal and depressed; was turned down by the live-in once and was bitter and angry; was eventually accepted to the live-in.

Ruel: molested by his uncle when he was six years old; parents always fighting; always felt different and was called names in school and even in martial-arts class; met a Christian and learned how to forgive and love; never had sex with a man but temptation is always there.

It is time for Vern to share his story if he wants to, and he does: from Utah; grew up Mormon and Lutheran; went gaybashing with a friend when he was a teenager and was shaken up by it; was turned in to the church and school when he turned down a suitor's advances; was sent for counseling and shock treatments; church and counselors told him to get married; was married for thirteen years with six kids; unbeknownst to him, his wife was telling people that she was married to a gay man, hence was ostracized; was set up and defamed by yet another rejected suitor; wife divorced him and took his kids and told them about his homosexuality in spite of a court order; making new life; struggling to overcome homosexuality and dating a new woman who is supportive.

Tonight, the sixtyish Worthen, who looks not unlike a kindly Christian uncle, is using the group's testimonies to explain how we fall into homosexuality and what can be done about it. It seems that there is an identity transfer that happens from father to son, mother to daughter, that is missing in a homosexual, so homosexuality is a search to replace that identity, Worthen explains. "Homosexual sex is not about sex but about the need for love and acceptance by someone of the same sex. The best thing we can do is to reaffirm our identities with our biological parent of the same sex, but as men, we can give each other this affirmation. We need to have relationships with straight men and to be accepted by them."

Worthen very strongly advocates the live-in program, which he says has a success rate of 50 percent. Much of the meeting involves extolling the virtues of the live-in program to Vern, though it isn't that hard a sell. Vern is happy as a bug simply to have found a group who readily understands his struggles and matches his horror stories pound for pound.

Why don't you show Vern the apartment, Worthen instructs Jim, and off the two trot to look at the space. All roads point to the live-in. The meetings always consist of a number of former and current program members who spend a good portion of their time sharing how much the live-in helps them. Even in the literature and the Xeroxed testimonies of folk who have overcome homosexuality, the live-in plays a significant role. My favorite personal testimony is from John Paulk who used to be a drag queen named

Candi, but one night on the dance floor of a disco, John/Candi looked to the mirrored ball and had a little tête-à-tête with God, saying, "I know you can help me. Some day I'll come back to you." John is now married to Anne and they live in Oregon, thanks to residential program 1988.

The drop-in group has a success rate of 25 percent. "What you need to do is to go to church as much as possible, go to fellowships and youth groups and Bible studies, surround yourself with Christians," Worthen advises a drop-in participant. "But you really need the live-in," he adds.

Being a church groupie was what Worthen himself did since there weren't any live-ins or support groups in his day. "Free of gayness" for some twenty years, Worthen said that when he first started his journey, there weren't ex-gay support groups, so he told many church members of his struggles asking them to pray for him. At the same time, he went to church social groups and prayer meetings at every opportunity. "If the church was open, I was there," he says. Soon, he found he "didn't have the urge" anymore, and when he did, he was reluctant to act on it for fear that the shame would show on his face. "I didn't think prayer would work. I thought that this one would be too big for God," Worthen chuckles. Worthen and Anita now work diligently to spread the message of healing homosexuality.

But what about the other 50 percent of the live-in group and 75 percent of the drop-in group that are not successful, what becomes of them? I ask Worthen, but he doesn't hear me. "The church should be a healing place, but instead it has become a judging place," he continues. "Mainstream churches say gays are okay, fringe churches say that gays are evil, so para-churches have to rise to up to help people like us heal."

There have been a number of horror stories that surround the live-in programs. Take the case of "Kathy." Persuaded to join the program by her family, she went through the usual rigamarole of ex-gay thought. The fact that she had been sexually abused was constantly used to explain her lesbian tendencies and her "hostility toward men." After she was kicked out of the program for resisting, the program members and leaders continued to call her on the telephone repeatedly, either to chastise her or to offer encouragements that she can still be heterosexual.

Most often, participants find the constant scrutiny and the lack of privacy hard to take. While these may be extreme examples of overzealous program leaders, there is a more subtle and perhaps more painful effect of the program, the psychological toil inflicted on the individuals.

Ask Sean Greystone. In 1994, he moved from Montana and checked into the San Rafael facility, then run by Love In Action. Five months later, he left the program.

Coming from a reasonably conservative Christian background, Greystone felt that he couldn't be gay and Christian at the same time, and, believing that, the only option he had was to change. "They hold out that apple to you, that 'we can help you change,' but they can't," Greystone says. "And you don't find that out until you go through a pretty miserable experience."

Greystone thinks that the program was perhaps a little better when it first started out, but now, it has gotten too militaristic. Over the years, Greystone charges, the program has constantly revised methods, making guinea pigs out of the participants to try out new methods and ideas, and adding more rules and more restrictions. And you can't question the teachings. If you do, they will tell you that you're being rebellious and then they throw you out.

"The abuses that I started to witness, the extreme manipulation and control from day one was getting increasingly more and more ridiculous," Greystone says. "A person is expected to give up all their rights, and do everything the leadership says without question. There is some severe psychological abuse that happens there."

What happens to the other masses who do not succeed in the program? They blame themselves for failing when it was the program that was never all that reliable in the first place. Many of the people who enroll in these programs are already in anguish over their lives, and the program just makes a further mess of people, he says.

Out of the sixteen people in Greystone's year, only four went on to the program's second year. The program is advertised as a one-year commitment, but Greystone says, "Once you get there, it's a two-year thing. In the middle of the first year, they will start pushing you to stay for the second year, and if you don't, they tell you that you're leaving God and you're bound to fail."

Now, at the age of thirty-two, Greystone lives in San Francisco and is "at peace with himself," independently studying and researching his spiritual life, and he no longer takes it for granted that "the church is right."

But why shouldn't a person who is profoundly unhappy with being gay not change that? Greystone points to the source of the unhappiness. "The people I met in the program weren't unhappy because they were gay, they were unhappy because the church said they couldn't be gay.

"The program says they can make you straight, that there is

freedom and there is hope, but the only thing they change is your behavior. You're gay going in, you're gay while you're there, and you're gay when you leave, you're gay even though you don't act on it," he says. "Nothing changes except that you have more guilt and more of a burden that you have failed."

Melvin Wong is a bespectacled fortyish man with graying hair. He is soft-spoken and he apologizes for the state of his office, he is in the midst of moving to a new office, and the small, elegantly decorated one-room office in the San Francisco financial district is temporary. When I first speak to Wong on the telephone, he boasts that he will probably be Exodus's official referral in San Francisco. He informs me that he has lectured on homosexual treatment issues in Taiwan, is on the psychology faculty of University of San Francisco (a Jesuit college) and works with something called the National Association on Therapy and Homosexuality. Later, I find out that Wong has never been on the faculty of USF.

He tells me that about 20 percent of his work deals with "gender issues" and that his success rate of helping gays become straight is "about 90 percent, depending on how much the client puts into it." A typical span of therapy usually lasts two to three years. And what does being cured mean? Wong compares it to a recovering alcoholic who sees a glass of wine—"There is a feeling but no urge to drink it."

Originally from Hong Kong, Wong is bilingual and many of his clients are Asians; he is proud to offer a cross-cultural perspective in his counseling. While he says that he "respects spiritual issues and will be sensitive to what is comfortable to the client," Wong admits that if moral values are called in question, he will fall on the side of Judeo-Christian values. Unlike most of Exodus's referrals, Wong has never been gay, nor participated in a homosexual lifestyle outside of his scientific research. He is married with a young daughter with whom he and his wife have taken the proper steps to ensure her heterosexuality.

"Family dysfunction leads to homosexuality," Wong declares. "A traditional family is important to gender identity formation. Sexual identity is the identity function of gender. It is how a girl knows how to be a girl and how a boy knows how to be a boy and that it is okay to be a girl or a boy."

All this apparently happens around the age of two to three-and-a-half. At that age, children need their autonomy from their mothers; girls need to separate from their mothers and then return, and boys need to find their fathers. Often, boys have a tougher time finding out their sexual identity because of the mother's protectiveness, hence "there are more gay men than lesbians, the ratio being about seven gay men to every lesbian," Wong reveals. Boys who have no "father hero" to emulate will be hurt and have a certain ambivalence in their sexual identity formation and will return to the mother. The motherly qualities of creativity and sensitivity are instilled in the sexually confused boy, explaining why gays are more creative and artistic and have higher than average language skills than heterosexuals.

"When one is confronted with homosexual feelings, there are two routes: affirmation (of those feelings) and true guilt," Wong tells me on my first session with him. He admits that he leans more toward the "nonaffirmation" route. In his professional opinion, Wong will ultimately advise that the homosexual lifestyle is not healthy. It leads to diseases and is psychologically unhealthy, he says. In fact, five years ago, Wong testified to that effect in front of the San Francisco School Board opposing Project 10, a drop-in counseling program for gay and lesbian high schoolers.

Interestingly, Wong's explanation of the root causes of homosexuality also explains that of homophobia. "Sometimes, a boy whose masculinity is not well developed will try to boost his male identity by becoming overtly masculine," Wong says. "The boy tends to be afraid of gays and becomes homophobic and can be a gay-basher."

Every homosexual has his own set of major circumstances, Wong says. In my case, the dynamics of the Asian family don't help either, with the "absent, aloof" father and the "overbearing, hysterical, overprotective" mother.

Wong's questions are strange, if not unsettling: "Were you teased for any difference? Did anyone laugh at you because you were different? Did your brother ever beat you up?" He tells me that assimilation and immigration can be trauma enough to cause dysfunctions in the family even if the tensions are not patently obvious.

He ends the session by telling me that he has a "strong hunch" that "a big trauma" occurred when I was between three to six years old. Wong clarifies his hint toward childhood sexual abuse by telling me that for many gay men, there was usually an episode of sexual molestation, sexual playfulness, or sexual stimulation that is against the child's will or without the child's knowledge—often somewhere between the age of six and ten. Eighty percent of lesbians have been raped at some point, he adds.

The numbers Wong cites are impressive if a bit questionable. But it is understandable how numbers can be comforting, too. Exodus and its various ministries keep a strange log of numbers and statistics. Given a ready outlet by their self-published books and pamphlets, they cite figures that beef up their cause. Sample:

—Roughly 80 percent of individuals involved in homosexual behavior come from homes where the father was a substance abuser or addicted to some other behavior. (from *Teens and Homosexuality: A Critical Time for Intervention*)

—Homosexual men are six times more likely to attempt suicide than heterosexual men.

—Between 25 to 33 percent of homosexuals are alcoholics (the national average is 7 percent). (from *A Biblical Response to the Pro-Gay Movement*)

"Gays are sexualized individuals, who confuse sex and intimacy, and are subconsciously trying to remake the past by controlling the present." Wong's couch manner is unnervingly gentle, and he is constantly offering little affirmations of how courageous and how honest I am to face my unhappiness with my lifestyle. The realization that homosexuality is a social disease is the first step to repairing the bonds and restoring my sexual identity, he offers encouragingly.

Wong's notions of homosexuality lingered with me long after I left his office. His suspicion that I was somehow fondled surreptitiously is a bit unnerving and is the stuff repressed false-memory cases are made of.

"I have a deep empathy for people who have to leave the gay lifestyle." Wong takes a deep breath and sighs. "I often find myself apologizing on behalf of the evangelical churches who are unaccepting of gays. It really isn't their choice to be gay."

"We are called Overcomers because we can overcome temptation with God's help. These struggles are put there for us to overcome." Fresh from a liver transplant five months ago, Ron Sharp, a portly charismatic man, runs Overcomers.

The group takes its name from the second chapter of Revelation where the Apostle John writes to the seven churches in Asia. Each letter ends with an admonition that "he who shall overcome" will be promised lots of yummy treats in the hereafter. Overcomers is a relatively new group to the ex-gay milieu. They are not on the referral list of Exodus nor were they listed as an organization that has applied to be one. I was referred to them by its leader's friend, who runs an Exodus-approved support group in San Leandro. This is a fringe group of a fringe group.

Overcomers is unique in that it is the only group that meets in the belly of the beast. Held every Thursday in a member's apartment in San Francisco's Sunset district, Overcomers is more a Bible study than anything else. There are no tawdry tales of temptations failed or fulfilled, no inspiring tear-jerking testimonials, only the stern reading of the Bible, where each verse is read, discussed in its context of finding guidance in "overcoming the life." There is no need for warm fuzzy self-help psychobabble or self-help books. The Bible is all they need.

In attendance today are Pete, who's brought his guitar so that we can sing some praises; Steve, a pastor's kid; and Al, who owns the house we're meeting in. Al's young daughter runs around the apartment; "Bible study is boring," she declares, before her dad chucks her in her room. Two other members, a man and a woman, are not here today. The group is starting the New Testament gospels afresh, having just finished a portion of Romans.

"Part of true faith is overcoming," Sharp tells the group, and we nod in agreement. "What we have here is a battle. It is a test. The question is, are we going to stand to the end?" Overcomers is decidedly more charismatic in its nature than New Hope.

When we get to the passages in the book of Matthew where King Herod, fearful of the wise men's message that the new King of Jews has arrived, calls for the slaughter of all newborns, the group's discussion takes one of its many tangents.

"I think Herod was possessed. That man was plain possessed!" Steve queenily exclaims.

Sharp agrees. "A lot of people are possessed by the spirit of the Antichrist, like Planned Parenthood and the Supreme Court."

Pete tells of how there's a store south of Market that's called the "666 store" with 666 paraphernalia. Al is concerned that his daughter is constantly bombarded by the messages of the Antichrist—like how at the local zoo, right by the monkey cage, there is a plaque explaining the theory of evolution. Steve wants to know if the Jews today are *still* God's chosen people as it says in the Bible. "If curses are brought on several generations, are blessings the same way?" Sharp tells him that they still are. Steve looks a little nonplussed.

The word "gay" was hardly ever uttered, and the question of homosexuality was seldom, if ever, raised in the meeting even though that is the main reason why we are gathered. All references to homosexuality are coded. "There is a politically correct line that says that you cannot get out of 'the life,' " Sharp says. "The main issue is guilt; how you will be when you stand before the

Lord. It is not whether you can be free but whether you want to be free."

Exodus International recently celebrated its twentieth anniversary, and the ex-gay movement is growing fast. They hold large regional and national conferences, and many members and leaders in the ex-gay movement take full advantage of the McCulture circus of America, appearing on many talk shows and call-in programs.

Still, ex-gays and their ministries find themselves in a strange limbo. Not all churches accept them or want to be associated with them.

"If you walk into a Christian function and say 'I'm a recovering homosexual,' they would clear the room," says Anthony Falzarano, leader of Transformation Ex-Gay ministries in Washington, DC. Conservative churches are embarrassed to have homosexuals on the property and liberal churches fear that ex-gay ministries will provoke a backlash from gay church members.

Some ex-gays have simply exchanged one closet for another. Whom to tell that one is ex-gay and how to tell them is a very pressing issue within the movement, and a lot of paper and time is spent advising how to "come out" as a recovering homosexual.

All these lead to ex-gay trauma #3: the ex-gay plateau. There is grave concern in the movement that being ex-gay is fast becoming, for many ex-gays, a subculture in itself. Ex-gays are sexually celibate but homosexuality is still central to them: Everything in their lives revolves around homosexuality and avoiding it. Listening to Exodus conference junkies and ex–program members speak, it is easy to see how this subculture is maintained.

Ultimately, the difference between gays and ex-gays is like the difference between cheese and cheddar. The ex-gays try to drown their homosexuality in Bible verses, marriage, family, and their own new subcultural niche, but their homosexuality remains.

Even the leaders of the movement have some doubts as to the validity of the organization's claims. Director Bob Davies and Lori Rentzal in their book *Coming Out of Homosexuality*, a classic in the ex-gay milieu, say that a change in sexual orientation is *not* the goal. The point, rather, is to have an intimate relationship with Christ and to be transformed by him. It's disturbing to realize that these Exodus groups know that the best they can do is suppress a person's sexual orientation, and yet they offer an entire industry catered to curing homosexuality.

When I first started going to these groups, I thought it would be a hoot to see what kinds of deluded wackos these people were. But as the weeks went by, all I saw were very unhappy people, people who have been so wrecked by their perceptions of what "the gay life" is, helped along by the decidedly homophobic rhetoric of "ex-gay" ministries.

I had decided that I had gone to enough meetings when a strange cocktail of anger and sadness started to seep out of me: I was close to a wreck when my boyfriend picked me up after what I had decided was to be my last meeting. Being gay is not easy, given societal objections and long-held prejudices. Heck, being straight or Christian is probably not easy either. But what was really deplorable was how these support groups exploit a person's failed relationships and dysfunctional family history as fodder for their spiritual and psychological bigotry. There are certainly plenty of heterosexuals who lead unfulfilling lives, with sad relationships and equally horrid family histories, but nothing says that these folk's misery is due to their sexual orientation. And if there isn't enough or suitable trauma, they simply suggest some and goad the person into a state where anything and everything is cloaked in sexual sinisterness.

The scary part of it all is that, at some point, I even started believing their rhetoric of why I was gay and the suggestions of trauma even when there weren't any. *Just what was my aunt doing with me in the carport, when I got my dick caught in my zipper when I was six?* I found myself thinking. The talk they give is that powerful. The combination of damnation and acceptance, the promises of a renewed self-esteem, and the threat of dire failure is intoxicating.

It is not a secret that the founders of Exodus International, Gary Cooper and Michael Bussee, have disassociated themselves from the group. The two men fell in love and left the organization they founded even though the organization still chugs along merrily, getting progressively larger each year. Of the organization they founded, Cooper and Bussee now have this to say: "Exodus is homophobia with a happy face."

Q-PUNK GRAMMAR

In 1994, in the midst of the hoopla surrounding the twenty-fifth anniversary of the Stonewall Riots, I did a radio interview with a journalist who was preparing this mondo piece on just that. He needed an Asian (any ethnicity), and I thought it might just be an interesting experience. The interview went along fine until I said the phrase "black and Puerto Rican drag queens." That's when the entire interview went sloshing downhill. "No!" Mr. Journalist declared. "That's a myth, and I want to debunk the myth. I want to tell the *Truth!*" He whipped out pie charts and little flow charts that illustrated his point; he said that he had interviewed at least six different people who claimed they threw the first brick. "Besides, the Stonewall bar did not allow non-White patrons or drag queens into it, so they couldn't have been there. They came the second night." Mr. Journalist beamed triumphantly. He had done this before. Then came the icing on his cupcake: "Knowing that, how does this change your opinions about Stonewall?" he asked smugly.

In retrospect, my answer was quite lame: "History is a matter of opinion," I said. "Different people will view history differently. I don't think who started it makes any difference, and I don't think it changes what was achieved and what was lost."

Thinking back now, it strikes me that I never understood Stonewall at all, I simply got it off the back of a truck. I was told it was important (is it?) and that I had to be suitably thankful for it (am I?). But that's what history is all about, isn't it?

We know something of where we were and the way we were, but where the hell are we going? Certainly gays and lesbians existed before Stonewall, were organized, and some even ran for office before Stonewall. I was way queer, and quite happily doing what queers do with other queers, before I had even *heard* of Stonewall. But those June nights in 1969, when I was a mere queer fetus, did something irrevocably incredible that cannot be denied. Still, time goes on, history is made, and history is lost.

The gay community is experiencing a great generational gap. It's a vicious cycle; each generation feels it has cornered the market on what it's like to be gay. The older generation tells us what it was like to be really gay *back then*, when they had:

- Donna Summer, when she meant something;
- Bette Midler, when she meant something;
- the good old days when punk was good and when a mosh pit was a mosh pit;
- real bell-bottoms, not $120 *Elle* magazine retro fashion;
- sex without condoms;
- venereal diseases that didn't outright kill you; and
- those insidious little homosexual mustaches.

My generation tells the younger queer brats what it was like to be queer *back then*, and how they will never know what it was like:

- to sit in a room of sixty people on a Wednesday night and try to reach consensus on something;
- to wear black-leather jackets with fluorescent queer-positive stickers, and how difficult it was to scrape those stickers off later;
- to be at a kiss-in when a kiss-in meant something;
- to be so filled with anger and a strange hope at an AIDS demonstration;
- having to defend using the word *queer*;
- when piercing our bodies meant something beyond fashion; and
- to make those damn 'zines, stapling and folding all night in the days before power staplers.

It's hard to live in the past, but still some people persist. Nostalgia bites hard. The old refuse to grow old, the young refuse to grow up. Maybe it's understandable. We don't want to grow old in a culture that doesn't value age, we don't want to be less than what we feel we're worth, and we cling to the best days of our lives. For some, it's the sixties, or the seventies. I find myself watching eighties music videos on MTV and tearing up. We want to forever be nubile young brown bodies, lying in the sun, glorious as a Whitman ode, succulent enough to make the boys we secretly love forget to say their prayers.

I look in my closet and I see that I have inherited a gaggle of colored drag queens (though some would still disagree over their color) tossing bricks at cops who look suspiciously like uniformed queens in a leather bar ten or twenty years later. I have inherited torrid stories of poppers and nights of unsafe sex in bathhouse upon bathhouse, each succeeding one more fanciful, more sleazy, and more capable of fulfilling every homosexual fantasy. *But you will never know what it's like to have fifty men stick their dicks in all your orifices every day of your life, will you, sonny boy?* I have inherited a virus, a wrecked community, memorials and Names Quilts, clinical trials and the AIDS industry as a viable and "noble" career choice.

But here I shall make a break: Let the young ones be queer the way they want to be queer, as long as they are queer, as long as they find among themselves each other to love. I've given up the dream of the Queer Nation. Race, class, gender, ideologies, and values will always divide us. It is ludicrous to think that since we share a common passion, we should all want the same things out of this life. We are each other's angels, and we are each other's demons. Beyond ourselves, there will always be those that wish for nothing more than to see us dead: They have been wishing and acting on it for centuries, but we are not vanishing. Call it sheer luck, call it divine intervention, call it tenacity. The fundamentalist Christians will call it a symptom of the end of the world as prophesied.

I have no idea what it is to be gay or queer anymore; nor do I care. I am so over being queer, and I don't care what I call myself or what anyone else calls me; it's all a matter of convenience these days. I believe in being unapologetic for my desires. All I know is when I wake in the night to find my lover's body next to mine, no history—real or imagined, myth or fact, inherited or created—can make me feel any less than brilliant in his arms.

CURRENCY

"It's always about money," my grandmother said. Every family fight and feud that I grew up witnessing was about money. How much was left, how much could be used, how much was taken advantage of, who was left out of a share.

I grew up quite suitably upper middle class. After five years of saving, borrowing, and hard work, my family managed to move from a dingy shophouse overrun with rats and centipedes at the back of my dad's clinic and bought into a new development, frightfully expensive at that time.

My father was the first person in his family to graduate from university—medical school, no less. There is a picture of him in his graduation robe and mortar board, rolled-up diploma in hand; standing proudly grinning beside him are my grandmother and grandfather and my mom in her beehive. I was always told that he was terribly clever and had wanted to go on to a further degree, but, by then, my brother was already born, and he had to support his younger sisters and brothers through school.

The years living behind the clinic are a haze to me. I was still a little tot contentedly playing with Rupert the Bear. My folks, my brother, and I slept in one room; my three aunts slept in the other. But the place always seemed more crowded with uncles, cousins, and my grandmother, who visited often. The "New House," as it was referred to, did not hold much gravity in my mind. In retrospect, I probably didn't even know what the hell was going on. One day, my folks took me for a drive and we drove the familiar road to the beach, but then we took a detour and ended up at this huge frame of a house. It was two stories, had a massive garden, a slight spiral of a staircase, wood paneling, air-conditioning, and the promise of many, many rooms. I learned the words "dining room." But more importantly, there would be a Study Room. Education was an important factor in "being comfortable in life," we were always told. "We make sacrifices so that you don't have to." The Study Room was for my aunts, who were still going through school, but ultimately, they would be for my brother and me.

Money and status were always uncomfortable subjects growing up, and they continue to be. Dad is a general practitioner. An ex-boyfriend used to leer at me, making some snide and cutting remarks about how I was nothing but a rich kid who had everything I wanted, Dad's occupation informing his ideas. But in Malaysia, and in Kuantan where my dad works, a regular GP is so unlike the doctors in America who charge exorbitant consultation fees. When my dad started his clinic in Kuantan, he was one of maybe two or three private practitioners. In twenty years, he and my mom (and the very same receptionist all these years) built up a practice with a loyal patient following. In some cases, he's been the family doctor for three generations of the family: The children that used to be brought by their parents now bring their children. There is very rarely a consultation fee, and the money is made in the dispensary run by my mom. Maybe $10 to $12 ringgit ($4 to $5 US dollars) a patient. Nothing made Mom and Dad happier than when a flu virus befell a family of six.

The funny thing is that I never felt like I grew up with money. More than money, we grew up with a strange sense of privilege and expectation. We were always reminded that we were "doctor's children." We were expected to get excellent grades, be supersmart, and become doctors (preferably), lawyers, architects, or engineers. Classmates in school whose parents weren't doctors, lawyers, architects, or engineers looked at us with a certain awe. Sure, we were more well-off than some other folks but not as well-off as others, but then again, doesn't everybody fall into this pattern? We were always urged to save, to be thrifty, to spend money wisely.

My parents, like practically all Chinese parents, believed in a good education for me and my brother. They believed that we should not have to go through what they went through, and they lived in fear that we might go hungry. So they spared no expense, working day and night to provide for us. But as comfortable as I was, there were always so many other kids in class that had pools in their backyards, their own rooms, yearly trips to America and Europe, and the latest electronic gadgets and games. I was always envious.

At the same time, my family could still afford to hire even poorer folk who attended our same church to help with the cleaning. I remember a friend's amazement that we sat to dinner with "the servant." His eyes widened in horror and amusement. In his house, he explained, the servant eats in the kitchen. Somehow, I think we never figured out the whole idea of hired help. For the ones that worked out, we always looked at them as a sort of family friend. When my maternal grandmother got older and more arthritic, my mom hired an older woman who worked as a road sweeper (which we were often told was one of the lowest occupations one could descend to; the caution: "If you don't study hard, you'll become a road sweeper/taxi driver, then you'll know!") to help out with a bit of cleaning and doing the grocery shopping. There are days when Mama-Chou and Ah-Sim would be lying on the floor eating peanuts and gossiping and watching daytime soap operas (with my grandmother translating inaccurately).

A few years ago, there was a news report on the front page of the *San Francisco Chronicle*. It proclaimed that gay and lesbian households were significantly richer than heterosexual households, since most often, both were working, and there was no family to support. That report, a national study, we're told, was reprinted and hailed as a milestone in gay and lesbian rights. We got an IKEA ad out of it, as well as a host of entrepreneurial products: rainbow-motifed wotzits all the way up the wazoo.

Similarly, we're told that Asian households in the United States make oodles more money than the other races, that they don't go on welfare like the other colored folks, that they are significantly wealthy, amassing riches starting from nothing.

What we're not told is that many gay and lesbian households simply eke by and that many Asian-American households make more money simply by the fact that there are two or three families living, working, and sharing a household, because asking for help and going on welfare is a horribly shameful thing.

What we get, then, is bitterness toward the Asians who "come over and make more money," a resentment toward Asian-owned businesses, when the business was bought through the graces of three families pooling their money together. What we get is the idea of special rights over civil rights. And what we get most is a seething loathing from our enemies, or those who we think are our friends.

Of course, "Asians" are certainly not a uniform race, but a convenient sociopolitical grouping of many different Asian ethnicities. And I must shamefully admit that some Asians can be as xenophobic and racist as anyone in this country.

Still, this I know: My dad and his older brothers put their younger brothers and sisters through secondary school and college. An extended family of uncles and aunts helped my parents put my brother and me through college. It wasn't a lot of money that they gave, but it was given, even in the toughest financial times. When my dad's younger brother visited San Francisco, we met up for drinks, and before I left, he pressed a few hundred dollar bills into my hand. I protested; he said, "When I was in school, your daddy gave me money to help, so it's okay that you take this, too." When I left for the United States, uncles, aunties, and cousins took me aside quietly and gave me red packets with money "to help out." When my cousin left to go to England to get a further degree, I sent her what money I could, too; it wasn't like I had that much money to fling around, and she certainly wasn't expecting it, but it was something that I deeply felt that I should do.

My mother tells me a story:

Her dad had been bilked out of the family timber business by his brother. To show he still cared and had some sense of family responsibility, his brother decided that he would give my grandfather a weekly allowance. My mom, being the youngest, was dispatched every week to go to my uncle's house to collect the allowance. She would arrive and be made to sit in the corner of their lavish living room and would be ignored for hours until my granduncle came and tossed her the envelope.

"It was so humiliating," she tells me. "That's why I want you get a good education and a good job so that these things won't ever happen to you."

Once, on her way back from school, my granduncle's Mercedes passed her and she spat at it. My granduncle saw this and immediately called my granddad, who caned my mom severely. "Even though he treats us like shit, you still have to respect him," he said.

My mother tells me this story one night and she admonishes, "When you don't have money, people treat you like shit, that's why we always tell you to study hard."

We're supposed to let bygones be bygones, but I can't forget being dragged to visit relatives during Chinese New Year, as is customary. We arrive at my granduncle's mansion, ring the doorbell, and wait at the gate. After a few minutes, his servant comes out and says that the family is not in, they're out visiting. In the car, my grandmother remarks, "But both his cars are in the driveway."

Recently, in the San Francisco *Bay Area Reporter*, one of the area's gay weeklies, an angry letter to the editor complained of an Asian-owned business in the Castro where he was treated rudely. "Perhaps they will feel more comfortable in Chinatown," the letter writer hissed. *They* want to take *our* money, but don't want to be respectful to us, he rants.

In this person's mind, and he possibly represents many, there is a *they* and an *us*. He feels that *they* treated him rudely because he was white? gay? Why else would he wish them to relocate to Chinatown? Is it then okay to be rude to white gays in Chinatown? We see each other and we don't see each other at the same time, and for those of us who live in more than one world, we perhaps see too much.

The samples and the methodology lie, they don't often tell the truth, whatever that may be, and we don't read between the lines enough before waving that new proof, new evidence that we can fit in the class that we feel we deserve to be in. The misreading of numbers and newsprint and the belief in them starts a frightening chain reaction. Sometimes I have this strange feeling in my gut: that the Left is very willing to forgo the Asian-American community in favor of the African-American and Latino/a communities; that Asians have to prove themselves as "people of color"; that gays and lesbians are growing increasingly hostile toward people of color.

In San Francisco, the head of the Log Cabin Club was a Chinese-American who actively spoke on behalf of the group. In one election, the only Republican candidate running for San Francisco mayor was a Chinese-American. A local city supervisor who is Chinese-American, though a Democrat, is often cited as the "conservative one." There are many Asian-Americans in the Republican party, locally and nationally. There are many Asian fundamentalist churches in the Bay Area. During the drive to oust the Boy Scouts from the San Francisco school districts for their exclusionary policies, and during the fight to implement Project 10, a counseling project for gay and lesbian teens, there were many Asian-Americans in the meeting halls opposing "gay rights." Sometimes I would like to think that the queer community has the ability to differentiate between individuals, between organized groups of a particular ethnicity and an entire ethnicity. But I can't be sure. I'm not even sure of myself: When I see or read Asians so wholly expressing a rabid conservative ideology, I do cringe inside of myself. Just as some more old-fashioned Chinese folks think I'm making the race look bad, I think the same of them. It's easy to want your communities to share your understanding of class values, of Asian values and of family values, but different people understand differently, we don't all think alike, nor should we.

I wonder how the man in that diner in the Castro who wrote the letter would have reacted if he got the same rude service but if the restaurant was run by Whites, or African-Americans, or Mexicans, or Cubans, etc. Would *they* still be taking *our* money? Perhaps I'm doing the same: unable to differentiate between an individual and a group, condemning the queer community on the actions of one silly faggot. But in the afterglow of the mass hostility toward immigrants in the state of California, I'm not sure if that man doesn't represent a large part of the queer community's attitudes, and whether the server's rudeness represents a large portion of antagonism toward the more privileged populace. The divide is great, and all we have to negotiate the chasm is a rickety wooden bridge of words, op-eds, media darlings and celebutants, and impotent politicos who aim for the lowest common sales pitch.

My great fear is that the Left, and the liberal/radical queer community at large, is fast equating Asian values with conservative values without as much as the blink of an eye.

I grew up and came out in the eighties, what is now known as the "me-greed-generation," the filthy stinking rich eighties. We had

Dynasty, Dallas, and other soap operas that glamorized wealth and demonized the poor. The poor characters in these soaps were always evil bitches and scheming bastards trying to get a piece of someone else's pie. My friend tells me that she used to watch *Dynasty* in a bar in West Hollywood; she enjoyed watching the queens want to be Alexis and Krystle. Back home in Singapore, being one of the women on *Dynasty* was also a fascination among the queens. They would assume names and characters and act out these people, remembering the bitchy lines and exchanging gossip about the stars. The allure of glamor and the idea that one could have so much money simply to fling away was terribly great.

The fascination with *Dynasty* among a lot of gays is interesting. First, many of us wished Alexis was our mother; she was powerful, had tacky outfits, and was accepting of her gay son. But deeper than that, through that soap and its camp sensibilities (*Dallas* was way too down-to-earth), many gays lived vicariously in this fantasy of power and wealth and upper-crust living.

Another source of our fascination with *Dynasty* was that it was just so campy. Everyone on that show was in drag, and only the queers managed to see that. Drag has always been a strange thing for me. I have some unresolved feelings about it. Not because of the effeminacy of it. I do admit that sometimes, it can tumble into the terrain of misogyny, which I do not care for. There are nice drag queens, and then there are really mean-spirited drag queens, who will use race, class, and gender for a cheap gag, a silly tittle. But what is most unspoken is that it ridicules and disparages what is seen as "trash." And just who exactly is "trash"? Then there is "rich trash." Even in the make-believe fantasy world of drag, wealth can't buy you out of your trashdom.

Drag is firmly rooted in the long history and tradition of camp.

In drag, the audience is asked to marvel at the kitsch, the send-up, and the ludicrousness of it all. But at the same time, we laugh and unquestioningly we are laughing at some very real and valid appearances in a certain realm and a certain culture. A polyester suit may seem silly, but for someone it may be the only good suit he has; a velvet painting, or an airbrushed scene of Waikiki on denim may seem so utterly crass, but for some folks, they mean a lot and are real decorating items, not campy artifacts. Laugh if you may, but know when to stop, too.

Here, we have class status and difference as defined by decor and accessories. It goes beyond good taste and bad taste. And besides, these style and taste judgments are rooted in the profoundly abrasive worlds of class diffrences.

In Jennie Livingston's *Paris Is Burning*, a young black drag queen looks at the camera, purses her lips, and says, "I want to be rich, I want to have a rich husband who will take me places and buy me expensive things . . . I want to be a rich spoilt white girl." There are drag queens in Asia who enter contest after contest in search of glamor, a sense of belonging, looking for that metaphoric "whiteness." Rich and white equals power and a preferred class status. Once, I said, to a friend's annoyance, that gay white men must be the most bitter people in the world: Here they are told that white men own the world, but simply because of their sexual orientation they are ostensibly denied easy access to this realm of "power," whatever that means these days. So we're told that gay rights are important, and we're asked to fight fight and fight for it. But when there are gay rights, people of color will still be people of color and women will still be women and they'll still be fucked while the happy white fags run off to the disco. My friend said I was being divisive. Gay rights are important, but it does not end there. Our gay leaders, pundits, writers, and activists will package and present issues to us, wrapped in hype and hyperbole and rolled out in endless magazines, newspapers, and talking heads. We need to rethink the packaging our struggles come in. We need to look at these issues and understand how they affect us, how they are intertwined with other issues and other peoples, and what we truly believe in and not just accept them off the tray.

I, too, wanted the glam life. I was dating this aerospace engineer from France when I was seventeen. He was stinking rich and he drove a Porsche, lived in a luxury penthouse apartment, and had all kinds of really expensive things. I was so taken by all those trappings. I loved walking in his house and simply taking it all in. But up to this day, what I remember most about our time together was him thinking I had stolen his Cartier lighter and his laugh when he saw that I had misset the silverware and fouled the table setting for his dinner. Thinking back, as one can only do in times like this, I wonder about what was going on in that whole situation. I simply wanted to be a rich spoilt white girl, too.

The thing called class is a weird thing; it seems that you're trapped in it and you can't buy your way out. And even if you do, possessions and wealth do not equate to class status—*that* is attained in ways I still do not possibly comprehend.

Something that never occurred to me before:

I was enrolled in a pretty prestigious school. (Pulled strings: Uncle was vice principal, hence skirted grueling application processes.) Each standard (or grade, if you Yanks so please) was divided into ten or more classes. Every year, based on our final examinations, we were either promoted or made to stay in the same standard. The final grades were tabulated and the forty highest scores went to the A class, the next forty to the B class. It was a matter of prestige to get to the A class, of course. The J, K, L, or M classes were for the kids who everybody knew would not amount to much. Most of the times, these classes and the kids in them were synonymous with the term "Chinese-educated," which was synonymous with lower-class, uncouth. The kids in the upper classes were synonymous with "English-educated," which was everything Chinese-educated was not. There were Chinese-educated kids peppered through the top classes, but these were few and they stuck together, were disdained by the English-educated kids.

I never realized how, even as a young pup, the structures that I grew up in segregated us. Class is all around, and sometimes, we don't see until it is too late. Then again, even had I known these structures and were aware of them, I really don't know how I would have lived differently.

My parents did not let me want for anything. They made sure I had all my basic necessities: food, clothes, shelter, education. They also believed in saving money, in being thrifty, in a good saving, a good sale, a good discount, in not being frivolous.

Being the first person in generations to break out of one class and into a more privileged one is a very strange thing. It is very much like immigration and exile: Unless you're there for a long, long time, you remember too much of where you came from. You start to get nostalgic, you start to describe so you won't forget, you visit a lot and think that maybe one day you will return, but most of all, you realize that too much of your body is invested in too many places, too many memories and warnings flow in your blood. You never really fit in, you're always a stranger in a familiar land. You can try to pretend, you can be comfortable in your disguise, no matter how brilliant it is, but you know you still can't buy your way out.

You know that the next generation and the next will be the ones who will really fit in, who will clearly define that break. Negotiating the spaces between classes is a terribly tricky thing. Some of it depends on one's personality and moral sensibilities. A lot depends on where one has come from and what one has learned in that span of life. Looking back on what I have just written, I realize that perhaps I have romanticized it all a little too much, taken way too many liberties, and I probably will continue to do so through my life. Romanticizing, of course, occurs when one is moving from one class status to another, or in transition, and is forced to look back. Maybe the sights in the rearview mirror are not so much romantic, but more incomplete, unfamiliar, hesitant, yet demanding of one's full attention. The move, this transition, may take years, generations, more than one's lifetime to accomplish. You can't just load the U-Haul and get there. And along the way, you will find a babble of voices: others, based on their own situations, who will tell you where and what you are whether you choose to believe it or not. It is crucial to know that class is hereditary too in a way, and that it changes so much from one generation to another, that it is ever evolving even in one's own life. For many of us, this state of transition *is* our class status, it is not as simple as checking a box on a tax form, and it certainly goes beyond earning potential.

In speaking about class, we are forced to look more deeply at our identities. Class is inexplicably contained within our understandings of sexual orientation, ethnicity, and gender. It also influences how we see the world and how we want to change it or not, and how much we feel we can. And with identity politics, this realization can either free or cage a person.

It is important that we impart some sense of our class values to the next generation or to the people who may be at similar crossroads. We need to leave better records that these conversations, these discussions, and these arguments about class in our communities happened, so that the discourse on identities, on class and race and queerness can evolve and move on to another, hopefully, more positive place. Understanding one's identity is a process and I look back on the civil-rights movement, the ethnic-studies strikes, Stonewall, all those marches on Washington, ACT UP and Queer Nation; those bits of memory, records, and history, blended with literature and art, have given me much raw material. With this, I can better articulate who and what I am to the people who would rather I did not exist.

MY FISSURECTOMY

Anal fissures are common enough, and they occur in many people, but when a gay man gets it, people start to act weird, and their eyebrows start to rise in insinuation and innuendo. Their minds, especially the straightest and the most conservative ones jump-start into speculation and the most unsavory innuendo. For the record, I wish I got it by butt-fucking, because *then* it would probably be worth it.

So, I've checked into the hospital for a quick snip. The procedure went as smoothly as possible for a patient who had seen *The Exorcist III* only two days ago on cable. The scene where the devil kills all those people in the hospital was fresh on my mind.

Everything was fine when I was discharged. I felt strangely all right even though I had been through some minor surgery. I felt like renting movies for the night, going to Boston Market for dinner, and maybe even having an extra chocolate fiesta. I was fine and dandy until the last bits of the epidural wore off at about midnight. Then it felt like there was something in my ass.

Do you know that feeling when someone you're really hot for has fucked your butt really long and hard? Well it feels nothing like that. It feels like there is an eternal fight between good and evil in my ass. This is how I cope with the pain in my ass. I imagine that there are three elves who live in my ass. Kiki, Rupert, and Chunks. They are the Colon Elves. They are kind of like the Smurfs, but more dusky and fibrous. Maybe like the Chipmunks but not as musical and with regular voices. Usually, they get along fine, living in harmony with the elements, and visiting each other with bags of Pepperidge Farm Milano cookies, but most of all, they just love having picnics. But sometimes they have wild adventures, too. Like the time the elves went off in search of hidden pirate gold after Chunks found the treasure map but they had to do it hot on the heels of a bunch of evil thieves who wanted nothing more than to snatch the gold from the elves' little hands. The trail was long and hard and, guided by that tattered map, the elves had to solve clue after clue along the way to help them on to the next step, and . . . wait a minute, that's the Goonies, not the Colon Elves. The Colon Elves do have wacky adventures, they're just too modest and reserved to talk about it much.

This is how I deal with the pain while waiting for the painkillers to kick in. I lie on the floor and imagine that I have been abducted by aliens and subjected to the Anal Probe. Then I have a terse exchange with FBI Agents Mulder and Scully.

"Agent Mulder, you believe me, don't you?" I'd ask with a plaintive look in my eye. And then Agent Scully would conduct an examination of my ass. Bent over on the examination table, I'd hear her say, "Mulder, come take a look at this."

"What is it, Scully?" he says.

"It's extraordinary." She frowns.

I try to look back. "What? What's happening?" I want to know the truth. The truth is in there.

Agent Scully looks at Agent Mulder incredulously. "Mulder, it looks like . . . elves."

"Scully, don't you see, the light fibrous texture of the fecal matter, the consistency of the blood, it all points to alien abduction. Why won't you believe, Scully?" Mulder drones.

"Mulder, I want to believe, but there are elves in his ass."

There is a videotape that helps parents potty-train their kids using catchy little songs. In the climactic scene, the little girl poops in the toilet all by herself and she goes down the stairs like a Miss Junior-Petite USA beauty queen (presumably she's wiped, but the video is vague on this) where she is greeted by her parents who reward her with a special song: "She's a Super Pooper Potty Pooper."

I never had such luxuries in life. No song and dance to cheer my bowel movements. My parents got me a small red potty. At least I *think* they bought it because I refuse to believe that it was hand-me-down like so much of my stuff. From the time I could sit upright till the time I could climb onto cold porcelain, that was my throne. I'd sit on it and read comics and watch TV. As a child, I developed a circular ring imprinted into my butt. When it was time to move to the porcelain, my folks snatched my little red pot away and told me that if anyone ever knew I ever used the red pot, they'd point and laugh and laugh and I would die from embarrassment and wouldn't be allowed to go to university and I'd end up a roadsweeper.

My proctologist is Dr. Robert Bush. He is a very competent doctor, a good surgeon with a wonderful and comforting bedside manner. But what the hell would possess a man to devote his life and a considerable amount of education to a field that makes him look up people's bottoms for the rest of his professional life? Sure, it might be fun for the first three or four hundred asses, but after that, it must be pretty tedious sticking your fingers and hollowed Plexiglas tubes into people and shining searchlights in—

"Oh," gasped Kiki. "Did you see that?"

"See what?" asked Chunks. He had just finished his third Pepperidge Farm Milano cookie, but he was still hungry for more of those shortbread cookies covered in a smear of dark chocolate and a thin layer of crushed walnuts, sandwiched together into one delicious cookie.

"That light," Kiki said impatiently.

"I saw it too," said Rupert. "I hope it doesn't spoil our picnic. The last time we had a picnic, that horrid rubber thing came out of nowhere and just kept ramming our picnic to shreds! And I spilt a cup of tea on my new Banana Republic shirt. It's ruined now. No amount of soaking could get it out, and now it's only fit for dishrags."

"Oh relax," said Chunks, cramming yet another Pepperidge Farm Milano cookie into his little elf mouth. "You're always seeing things, Kiki, like the time you said you saw a small mammal, not unlike a gerbil, you said, *not unlike a gerbil!* Now really! What would a gerbil be doing *here*, of all places?"

"I didn't say it *was* a gerbil, I said I saw something woolly and furry like a mammal," Kiki said crossly.

"Wait, there it is again," Rupert said. True enough, there was a thin ray of light hovering over the elves' very special picnic. Even Chunks was forced to put down his Pepperidge Farm Milano cookie to stare at the strange light.

The night after the procedure, my friend Lisa brings over a stack of Kotex Stick-on Maxi-pads (with wings) which I'll need because of the blood that is discharging from my butt. They're huge. I stick one on the inside of my underwear before going to bed and the next morning, when I wake up, it's stuck to my left armpit. How do you keep it in place, I ask her. She says, it's a skill you develop.

But I'm on the mend. Chained to the routine of fiber, Metamucil, fluids, wet wipes, sitz baths, and painkillers. In my family, we deal with pain and medical procedures with quiet fortitude, grit our teeth, and get on with life. My great-great grandfather carried on his church work even when leprosy had taken its toll; he'd lose fingers and toes on simple walks. To my horror and annoyance, my mother mowed the lawn two days after her hysterectomy. Aunt Esther toughed out her stomach cancer with colostomy bags and volunteer work. Cancer, arthritis, gout, snapped bones, infections. This butt thing is nothing. There're worse things ahead, and I know that. And every time I get sick, I think that this might be the year it all falls apart: This might be the year that I won't bounce right back; this may be the year that I'll be left uninsured; this will be the year that I will have to learn a new vocabulary to describe what is happening to me. That this will be a difficult year, chained to pills and blood work, insurance forms and prescriptions, X-rays and tissue samples. Or this will be just another year after all.

THE ENDLESS POSSIBILITY OF A KISS IN A FEVERED FARAWAY HOME

Homesickness, nostalgia, memory. A bitter wrench in my heart that reaches its little inexorable fist into my throat. Singapore 1987: The Singapore Film Society had acquired a print of *Kiss of the Spider Woman* and every art-fag, closeted or not, and then some, have shown up; a second late-night screening has been quickly arranged to handle the mad crush. For the art-fags, the draw was watching a decidedly homosexual movie and the scene where Raul Julia kisses William Hurt at the end, even though we all knew that that brief kiss had been judiciously snipped out by the censors. But we crowded in, we watched, we held our breaths at *that* point and as Hurt puckered up, all he kissed was a loud scratch and a bad edit. But in that brief unseen gap, we saw that kiss, and for many of us, it was deeper, longer, wetter, and more meaningful than the director, the actors, the writers, and censors had ever imagined. That strip of x number of frames lying on the Ministry of Community Development's floor was a slice of all our unrequited queer angst, love, joys, hopes, and dreams seething behind our ribs. A brief flash, a supernova of possibility seen only by a censor, those fortunate enough to go abroad or those who had access to black-market uncensored videotapes, usually taped directly off a screen at an American cinema complete with real-life Americans walking in front of the screen, popcorn in hand.

My folks took me and my brother to watch Disney movies when we were little. They were convinced of the educational quality of Disney movies, and they wanted for us to learn our English correctly. For a while, we lived at the back of my dad's clinic, which was in front of the Cathay cinema. Every evening, I would sit on the receptionist's desk and watch the throngs of people coming out of that night's movie.

A trip to the cinema back home is nothing like going to the movies in the United States. There, it's messy, noisy, there're bad commercials that everyone knows by heart, whole families come with children running amok, and there's plenty of munchies— various peanuts, Western and Japanese-style candies, fruits in little plastic bags. Sometimes, the subtitles (a combination of Chinese and Malay for English films, or English, Chinese, and Malay for Cantonese and Mandarin films) fill up a quarter of the bottom edge of the screen. The last time, I forgot to wear long sleeves and emerged from Stallone's Alpine adventure, *Cliffhanger*, with mosquito bites over my arms and face.

I love how people talk back to the movie screen back home. How little old ladies and plump moms would screech "Jagar Belakang!" or "Quick! Hurry Up!" at crucial nail-biting moments. At melodramas, it's not uncommon to hear tearful sobs of "No! Don't do it!"

In Bangkok, I once saw a dubbed version of Shelly Long's *Troop Beverly Hills*, where the witless Long plays a Girl Scout troop leader who helps her overprivileged but unhappy posse of Beverly Hills she-brats find their hearts and themselves through a series of implausible events. The great thing about the movie, dubbed into Thai, was that there were only two voices for women: an old woman and a young girl. So all the Girl Scouts had the same voice, while all the older women had one voice. It was storytelling at its postmodern best.

There is always a sheer joy at the movies, watching the kids and adults enjoy themselves so thoroughly. It's noisy and rambunctious and people get pissed off at each other and some get hushed a lot, but somehow, it's never like the time when I was at the Roxie cinema in San Francisco watching a Hong King movie. A man in the audience, probably on bad 'shrooms, decided that he had to guffaw at every grammatical error and typo in the subtitles. This he would do by repeating the subtitle quite audibly and then dissolving into a fit of hyuks. At first, people didn't seem to mind, but after fifteen minutes, it got tiresome and the audience was quite obviously annoyed and each waited for someone to tell that plonker to shut the hell up. Nobody ever did, though. At such times, I secretly wish I was a villain of a John Woo film with six-guns packed on me, able to blow that man's balls off in one sharp shot.

I once read that in a certain South American tribe, the medicine man would take his apprentices to a local cinema on their final leg of training. Movies, he tells them, are not unlike the visions the sick see just before they die. For me, movies are not unlike the visions the homesick see when their hearts are bearing the weight of the realization that they're homeless, exiled, or caught in a limbo between native and tourist.

When the lights go down and the movie begins, the fever flares. I find bits of home in hearing Mandarin spoken the way I remember, as I have taken it for granted, not used it, and lost large chunks of it; there's home in reimagining straight Hollywood plots as the queerest ones and inserting myself in the narrative; and there's plenty of home watching two guys kiss on the silver screen just as I have kissed the men in my life.

THE CRISPY EDGES
OF PANCAKES

Being Chinese in America, I often hear people tell me that I "come from an oral tradition." Actually, thinking back on my family, I must admit that this is true. We were always either eating or shouting at each other. We even managed to eat and shout at the same time. A formal dinner at a swank restaurant or a tasty midday snack would be marred by arguments about finances or any number of petty matters. You can't get more oral than that.

My parents and grandparents have this intense fear that the children in the family will starve to death. From my limited contact with the diaspora, I would even venture to say that this dread of starvation is the one major defining trait of being Chinese. It all has to do with living through the Japanese occupation, the race riots during the years following Independence, and other times when there wasn't enough food, I'm told. Likewise, my parents and grandparents lived in mortal fear that the children in the family would starve to death and become the scurvied, sad-eyed UNICEF poster children, held in some frizzy-haired blond has-been actress's arms as the extreme example of the cruel third world.

My maternal grandmother likes to cook a lot of food. She likes the reassurance of having leftovers in the fridge, bowls of cold food covered with a plate. Never mind if it sits there; the next day, she's cooking more. When Saran Wrap showed up one day in the local supermarket, she went mad cooking more and more food, comforted by the knowledge that this new clingy technology would preserve her home-cooked goodness to a moist perfection. When yet another one of those recessions that seem to come by as regularly as bank holidays hit, we tried to get her to save money by cooking less food. She did, but then she felt so bad that her grand-kids would be hungry, all day she'd ask us: *Are you hungry?* and during dinner, *Is there enough?*, followed by the declarative *See, you still hungry, I go cook an egg for you, okay?*

My grandmother says that my dad and his older brother, her two oldest sons, are short and stocky because they were born during the war: no food, nothing but potatoes, she says. The others, the seven others, were born after the war, that's why they're so strapping, so tall. If you want to grow big and strong, you must eat more, my other grandmother agrees with her. The reason why people in America are bigger than in China is because they have better food. All that beef and steak and potatoes is good, she tells me.

American food always held some sort of charm for us. My maternal grandmother was even able to believe that McDonald's was a terribly nutritious meal and was comforted that I was chowing at a McDonald's if I wasn't eating at home. My paternal grandmother remained unconvinced that anything outside of home-cooked meals could save her children and grandchildren from malnourishment.

To me, America meant bacon. Advertisements showed bacon on plates in restaurants; families on TV and cartoon characters in comic books ate it for breakfast. It all looked so foreign and so exotic. Sure, we had bacon back home, but it was horridly expensive and my grandmother always kept the damn thing in the freezer so it was sheer hell trying to make any of it without a huge production of chipping at ice and defrosting. Other than that, the bacon strips in Burger King's bacon double-cheeseburger didn't really fit the bill. It didn't even look like bacon, and, marred by the beef patty, ketchup, and mayo, it didn't even taste like it. Later, I found that it was really made of soy, not pig. It's funny how you can calibrate taste so accurately, to differentiate pig from soy-pig.

The sense of taste is closely related to the sense of smell. If you can't smell something, you can't taste it. This easy fact was quite useful when it came to gulping down the government-issued milk that I was forced to drink during my year in Primary 2 (second grade). The lumpy lukewarm milk mixture, bused in by the Department of Education, was actually meant for children who the teachers suspected were malnourished. But since the suspected malnourished children were far too busy playing catch or chatek during recess to bother about the government's efforts at fattening them up, the canteen lady in charge of ladling the lumpy gruel, needing to get rid of the supply, decided simply to force it down anyone who came by, even obese little me.

When I fall in love, I always seem to end up cooking for the person I'm smitten by. Once, there was a person whom I was so taken by I spent two days making a pasta sauce. The whole process involved grilling peppers of all different shapes, colors, and tastes on the oven rack for hours, then slowly stripping them of their skins. The denuded peppers, in all their squishy aromatic splendor, were then put, along with whole cloves of garlic and some turmeric, in a large earthenware pot overnight to undergo some kind of miraculous change rivaling the Miracle of Lourdes. Next, it was rescued and diced into a nice soft mush which was added to the frying mixture of minced garlic and onions, fresh basil leaves, a small sliver of ginger, a sprinkle of coarse black pepper, and random sprinklings of ground spices from the spice rack. The whole frying mixture was then introduced to a huge heap of finely chopped and diced fresh tomatoes and a small pot of tomato sauce. The whole sloppy mess was cooked, simmered, and cooked again.

When we finally sat down to dinner, I lied and said the sauce was really no problem at all, less than an hour, I said. If I told the truth, would he have loved me more? Otherwise, I'm calling my mother long-distance at ten-forty-five in the night, saying, "Mom! What's flan and how do you cook it? Where can I buy one?" Only to have poor Mom panicked, and demanding, "Are you taking drugs? What's wrong with you?"

The great thing about moving out and living on your own is that you can eat whatever you want and whenever you want to. No more sad surprises at dinner where you smell pork chops but discover broccoli, or see pork pie in the fridge but get heaps of macaroni and boiled chicken soup instead. If my mother and grandmothers ever knew what I eat these days, how I eat it, and how many meals I forget to eat, they'd weep.

There's this restaurant near my apartment that serves big portions of food. A single serving of home fries there is enough for a family of four for a week. What I love most about the place is their pancakes. For $3.50, they'll give you three pancakes, each slab the size of a dinner plate, the middle a thick mess that sops up the lump of butter and the syrup like a hungry horse's tongue, the edges crispy and slightly burnt. The best thing about these pancakes is that they somehow affirm that experience of making my first stack of pancakes. I fucked it up royally but still ate it in sheer arrogant delight. Sitting in that restaurant with my mug of all-you-can-drink coffee and that plate of pancakes, I feel good knowing that what is before me has not conformed to the rigid social configuration of the serving suggestion as pictured on the side of the box.

My greatest breakfast moment was when I discovered the best way to eat these slabs of pancakes. First, you never pour syrup all over them. If you do, the cakes simply become a dense sticky mess. Horrid to look at, worse to fork into your mouth. You smear the butter everywhere you can reach, though you should not use too much butter because the excessive oil will only make you sick. Having done that, cut a good bite-sized piece off the edges, drip a wee bit of syrup on the chunk on your fork, bring fork to your eager mouth. Eat all the edges. Forsake the middle. It's not worth it.

The thing about every singular dish anywhere is that there's always one thing that strikes you more than others, like the crispy edges of pancakes. The terrifyingly greasy chicken skin at Popeye's, the skin of charred salmon steaks, the wonderful clammy stickiness of glutinous rice wrapped in banana leaves, the way cheesecake sticks to the roof of your mouth. It's like everybody can have an intensely gourmet moment as many times a day as they want. It's these little bitty moments that we so often don't notice or appreciate that can make any meal, any snack, a small wonder.

I've got to try to keep my shirt on around the house when I'm visiting my family. It seems easy, really, but it's not. Not with my grandmothers constantly hovering over me, shaking their heads wistfully, and occasionally grabbing my arm to prove that they can encircle my entire bicep between thumb and forefinger. Sometimes, they even lift my shirt to look at my rib cage in an attempt to illustrate to anyone around how I'm all ribs poking out of my skin. *Pork bones, nothing but pork bones . . . you look like a starving chicken,* they shake their heads in sadness and worry.

I'm trying to keep my shirt on because I've gotten a couple of tattoos. It all would be fine except that some conventional wisdom in the typical Chinese family says that only gang members who are drug addicts or pushers have tattoos. It doesn't help that I also shave my head to a fine stubble, since prison wardens shave convicted drug addicts' heads.

I am nervous about growing thin. I'm walking around the house with my shirt off. My ex-boyfriend is visiting. He sees me and says that I've grown horribly thin. Later that night, I weigh myself— 120 pounds, the same as I have been for the last four years. I think that perhaps my flesh and muscle are simply shrinking away, disintegrating into themselves.

I know if I see my grandmothers or mother, they will be shocked and upset at how thin I've become. My grandmother will rush to the kitchen to make all my favorite dishes. Anytime any of the kids said that a dish was good, she'd cook that dish every day for weeks until we were totally sick of it. But for my mom, it's worse. A homosexual son who's thin can only mean one thing in her mind.

These days, I have a taste on the tip of my tongue. It is a familiar taste, one that I've grown up with, one that instantly ties me to where I stand now. Mere language can do little to describe it. How can it? How can a permutation and combination of *sweet, sour, bitter, salty, tangy, spicy,* and all those regular words that you may find, say in a recipe book, accurately describe the taste on the tip of my tongue?

It will take many words and more infinitely, a lot of the memories inscribed in my body to describe it.

Why do I bother? Simply because we've all had this taste. It may not be the same taste, but the process of discovering it and emblazoning it on our minds and our bodies is as important as breathing and eating.

The taste on the tip of my tongue is the taste of a plate of meatballs. Not any plate of meatballs, but one very special plate of meatballs that my paternal grandmother would bring every time she visited. The meatballs were freshly made, direct from my granddad's slaughterhouse to the meat grinder to my grandma's trusty kwali steamer on her woodfire stove.

What I loved most about the meatballs was that they sometimes were strung together by a thin membrane of meat. This always reminded me of the pictures I saw of sausages in children's books: the dog running with a string of bangers in its mouth, a whole long chain trailing in the wind, the dog's eyes and tongue full of sheer delight at its ill-gotten gain, the bangers fluttering good-bye to the fat chef waving either a meat cleaver or rolling pin in the background.

My grandma would show up, whip out a plastic bag of meatballs from her rattan market basket and make up a plate for me with a small stack of toothpicks on the side. She was always sure to stick at least two toothpicks in a few of the balls, an incentive to get me started. The best part of it all was that I was expected to eat every single meatball as proof of my gratitude and love for her.

The last time I was home, I offhandedly remarked to my grandma how much I missed the meatballs. She shook her head. The butcher from her old hometown had died. The butcher from Sungei Lembing, the little one-street tin-mining town where she lived until my grandfather died, had the best meatballs. No duplicating, she said. *No more yok-yin.* The next morning, I looked out the window and saw her tying on her padi-field hat and leaving through the cast-iron front gate. When I went into the kitchen at lunchtime, she had already returned from her trip. On the table was a dish of meatballs.

Apparently, she had gone out to the market and bought all the available meatballs. This I found out the next day when I went to the corner shop for breakfast with my dad. The woman selling the curried noodles yelled at my dad, *I don't have any more meatballs. Your mother bought all of them!*

People always ask me if I miss home. What I miss are particular things about home, and the thing that I miss most is the food.

I know how to cook. I know I can re-create that food in my

kitchen if only I can find the correct ingredients. But that's more difficult than it seems. I go to the supermarket. I push my cart up and down the vegetable aisle. I try to look for a certain vegetable. I can't find it. I don't know its English name. All I know is its folk name and what it looks like and that's really not enough to bother the $4.25-an-hour shelvers with. If not the lapse of naming, it's the difference in naming. My grandmother once taught me how to make *poh-pia*, a local favorite. *You use turnips*, I remember. But turnips 8,440 miles away are not the same as the scraggly bunch I'm holding up in the middle of the night in a Safeway. I'm going up and down the aisles trying to make the lines of memory, of taste, and the vegetable I see before me match up, but like a Vegas slot machine, it's a long shot.

I go with friends to a restaurant specializing in food from my homeland but somehow, the crudeness of the food I know so well on my tongue is lost. The fine ingredients and the expensive spices are all somehow different. A lot of it has to do with how water tastes different in the two countries, too. My friends don't mind: They have experienced the food of another land, they believe it is real, the experience re-created. I tell them about the subtle difference, but they're still happy that they've experienced the food of the Malaysian peninsula and they like it even though I think they've been swindled, conned by a trickster with a spatula who's taken their money and run.

But we take what we can wrap our tongues around, straining for our taste buds to cling to the tiniest thread of glutinous memory. Food is food; and we wave to the sad red-haired clown guarding the Golden Arches. Swallow the crispy edges of pancakes, remember meatballs, choke down the horrid, savor the incredible, pay homage to boyfriends we cooked for, who became emotionally

BLAH

Sometimes I think the only community I want or need is my cat, my friends, and their cats. (Oh okay, dogs can join, too.)

Sometimes I think that the need for "community" is the bane of the community.

Sometimes I have no idea what community means. Then I go to a demo, a street fair, or a parade, and I know again. And after a good hour of that demo, street fair, or parade, I'm sick of community and wish I didn't even know it in the first place.

Sometimes I think that I belong to too many different communities and that each intersects and overlaps like a messy ball of wool, clawed to death by a playful kitten. But at the end of it all, I love wandering around in the subsets, the byways, and the peripheries of these communities and I am damn happy that I feel at home in all of them.

Sometimes I think these communities wish I weren't in them.

Sometimes I think that community is a good excuse for not even attempting to have an identity of one's own.

And just because I'm in a particular community, it doesn't mean that we should do everything together, dress alike, think alike, hate alike, love alike, and accessorize alike. It's community, not some fucking junior-high pajama party.

Sometimes I think community is just another big sociopolitical pajama party, and is a means of compensating for all those junior-high pajama parties that we wished we were invited to but weren't because we were too weird/unpopular/poor/ugly, etc.

Sometimes I think that I don't belong to enough communities.

Sometimes I feel excluded from those communities that I'm told I should be in or that I'm told I'm in.

Sometimes I think it'll be nice to find just one good community to hang in. But heck, I'm such a greedy slut, and I know I'd probably want more.

Sometimes I wish we could all just get along.

Sometimes I don't want to get along.

Sometimes I think that communities need to be formed based not only on identity but more so on affinity.

Sometimes I think that there's no such thing as community.

Sometimes I take my communities for granted.

Sometimes I can't even speak about community without giggling, retching, getting nauseated, beaming broadly, being extremely proud, overtly fanatical, unbearably essentialist, yawning uncontrollably.

Sometimes I find comfort in community when I feel too displaced, too exiled, too far away from home, and too amputated.

Sometimes I look back on my years on this earth and over a life barely long enough to contain a good curse, and as I look over my shoulder to see the years of shouting and sighing and crying and mourning and fighting and ashes and laughing and grieving and witnessing and loving and hating and fucking and coming, I still think I don't really know what community is, where I fit in, and where I fall out. And in the midst of this queer diaspora, this Asian diaspora, an unapologetically queer Chinese-Malaysian tattooed punkish guy is daily negotiating the spaces between disclosure and safety.

ON ~~ASS TACTICS~~, ~~AZTEC TICKS~~, AESTHETICS

What does cultural aesthetics mean in a world that is changing rapidly, where identities and cultures are in flux, in the blender on frappé, where celebrity Buddhists and white Hindus run rock festivals to save the world, and where culture has become so commodified that you can assume another as easily as going to the mall, guided by last month's full-colored spread in *Elle*, *Family Circle*, or *Needlepoint Digest*? In the spirit of individuality and tolerance, assimilation and acculturation, the Suzie W(r)ong doll is repackaged and paraded as bitchin' Filipino-Irish-Cantonese-Alien B-girl rapper Suzie W.; as Suzie-StarChild, transgendered hippy-vegan militia guru; as Steve, gay Latino Republican for Choice in Deportation; as Suzan Whong, dressed as Pocahontas as Fa Mu-Lan as Miss Eskimo Hawaiian Tropic in fake fur bikini and Keds, pillar-box red Candies (panties are optional, of course).

Aesthetics was one of those words that I couldn't spell without the help of my spell-checker or my trusty American Heritage Dictionary of the English Language (three books for three bucks + postage, such a deal). Cultural ass-tactics exist in the same way that fleas of the dead family dog do, still biting after darling Fido has been crushed under the wheels of the biggest fucking lorry in the world, driven by Mr. Moto, the guy who used to be an accountant for Jacoby, Ramirez, Wong, Wong & Fonzirelli, until he discovered the sacred floating lotus within himself.

Cow-churrail aztec-ticks exist and they don't.

Cowlture means very different things to different people. Identity politics is a maddeningly individual thing, and the joy is finding others who subscribe to your particular lottery numbers and want to play with you at the next drawing.

We are influenced and informed by who and what we are, how we live, and how living is done around us. I am a queer Asian guy, a writer and performance artist, a first-generation immigrant, who came into my queerness in the Day-Glo soaked eighties. Obviously, what it means to be Asian in America, Asian-American, queer, part of the Asian diaspora, or any combo platter of those (no substitutions please, 49¢ to supersize soft drink and fries) will be different for me than it would for someone else even in the same straits.

The problems occur when audiences and arts administrators and programmers don't feel that I am playing the carl-cheer right. They demand yet another ethnic dance festival, another trip to the chink-o-rama with the big Ferris wheels, spinning Ethnic Mc-Nuggets in convenient packs of six, eight, or sixteen. Something to stick up on the shelf between the Michener books, the *Joy Luck Club* laser disc, and the souvenirs (oooh! big fan, rice-paddy hat, straw mat, sarong, sarong, sarong) from Asia-fest '95.

There will always be work that is deemed not queer enough for the queers, not Asian enough for the Asians, not Asian enough for the queers, too Asian for queers, too queer for the Asians, too much, too little, too bad. A tub of eels of fears and inadequacies to fill the *unagi-maki* roll of cultural consumption (comes with miso soup!), waiting for Goldilocks to learn how to use chopsticks (or at least ask for a fork, dammit, or use her fingers) so she can find the right morsel to take to the right BacoLounger before crawling into the right futon, dreaming of pork chops, bacon, and everything else Just Right.

Ooo. I'm having a thought: (serious voice) Cultural aesthetics is important as long as cultural politics is important, as long as identity politics have been a long hard-worn struggle and fight.

Cull-chew-real asstack-ticks? I'm not too sure what it really is anymore, but I do know that if you buy into it too much as an artist and especially as an audience, it can be severely limiting. It's good to know what you like from art, and what you identify with, but it's much better to be open to the sea of possibilities and the different, challenging, opposing discourses that you might find in there. Cultural aesthetics is a good starting point, and starting points are just that—hopefully they lead somewhere and the roads ahead are not filled with dodos (the extinct bird, not the idiots in our lives) running backwards. Remember to wait at least thirty minutes after eating. You may start when you're ready.

DEATH OF THE CASTRO

When I first came to San Francisco, all I knew about the Castro was that I had to find it. Using only one of those crappy tourist-bureau maps that I found in the drawer of the hotel, I set out in the March drizzle and walked down Van Ness, turned up Market, and, considering my less-than-competent map-reading skills, miraculously found my way to the Castro. I bought Alan Hollinghurst's *The Swimming Pool Library* at A Different Light Bookstore, ate at Without Reservations, and was hog-happy watching the homos come and go.

Since moving to San Francisco and living here, the Castro has rather lost its sheen for me. It is not the filth nor the dog poo smeared across a four-block radius. It is not the sight-seeing tour buses that trundle through, or the straight tourists clinging to each other for dear life and protection; nor is it that ripe brand of jaded

San Francisco ennui. Rather, I've discovered a horrible thing: The Castro is actually a very boring place.

There are better cafés and java joints in the Mission and the Richmond, better shopping downtown and in the Upper Haight, better walking in Noe Valley, better bars and clubs south of Market and in the Lower Haight, and better eating practically everywhere else. These days, I venture into the Castro to go to A Different Light, or the Castro cinema, to visit chums or to take visitors through it.

I do realize the historical significance of the Castro. But that's hardly enough to make a person want to hang out there, is it? I recognize that it is essential as a place where queers can gather, be "safe," an epicenter for queer demos and rallies and assorted community gatherings. But even taking these reasons, there are a lot of queer-bashings in that vicinity, I mean, if a queer-basher was looking for queers to bash, where better to go than to the salt lick? Queer demos and rallies are great, but how often do those occur? So what's left but block parties and the interminable Halloween thing?

The Castro has become a few blocks of expensive T-shirt and clothing shops, juice bars, yuppie eatery chains, and trendy neighborhood shopping and dining. Thrilling, huh? The merchants constantly complain about the street kids, the homeless people, and the flyers on lampposts. And then there's the old man with the obsessive-compulsive disorder who spends his whole day ripping down flyers posted on the lampposts. Whether it was a flyer for a party, a sex club, a lost person or belonging or pet, or a call for a town meeting, he just gets completely apoplectic at the sight of paper on vertical surfaces.

The anti-flyering hysteria of many Castronites is unfortunate.

In the interest of their idea of what a "clean" neighborhood should be, they've taken away a lot of the character of the neighborhood and its community. It is through these flyers that the denizens of this community communicate and tell each other where to find one another—in clubs, social and political meetings—and what's going on between us all.

I have very mixed feelings when people speak about the Castro excluding them and that they don't feel welcomed there. These have included people of color to women to women of color to "fat middle-aged" men. (One of whom accosted me on the street to berate me after I said in an interview that most people in the Castro can only tolerate Asians when buying takeout or collecting laundry. "Try being fat and middle-aged in the Castro," he snapped.) Still, somehow, there are many queers of color, women, and fat middle-aged men slinking around the Castro. And I wonder: Are they there because they're comfortable there or are they there because there's nowhere else to go? In any case, is racism a good reason to want in to the Castro, or is it a good reason to find an alternative to the Castro?

Somehow, I understand the desire to have a place to belong to, to go to feel "at home." But why does it *have* to be the Castro? It is not written anywhere that a queer absolutely positively unquestioningly *has* to go to the Castro, and like it.

The Castro does make many people feel at home and it is the designated queer epicenter for the nation. But it is possible to live happy, positive, and rewarding queer lives without the Castro, too.

Racist attitudes in the Castro exist even though many would rather turn a blind eye to it. Many still remember the Midnight

Sun debacle (triple-carding and alternative drink prices for people of color), while to many others, that is either a distant memory or was never an issue. A clerk at Headlines once told a visiting friend and me the price of a watch and added, "This isn't Chinatown, you know." We had neither commented on the price nor expressed that it was expensive, we just merely asked for the price.

It is unreasonable to hold a neighborhood responsible for the bigotry and stupidity of individuals. But there is something about the Castro that makes it this living, breathing being. The myth of the Castro precedes it, and people come to it expecting it to be some queer nirvana where lion and lamb screw each other in the butt, and pixies and fairies dance their sugarplum dance.

There is still a small part of me that longs for the Castro Street of March 1990 when I first stumbled into it. I long to be able to go through the two blocks in awe and in wonder of all things queer.

Like it or hate it, Castro Street will always be there for those who need it as I needed it all those years ago. But as one grows older, one learns more about what it is to be queer and perhaps one outgrows the things that once provided comfort. So, we leave it to make space for others who need it now while we go on to create new spaces for those who are queerer than our queer.

SLAMMED

The world is full of poems. Try editing a literary journal and putting out an open call for poetry, having a reasonably prized poetry contest, or hosting an open reading, and you will be besieged with poets and poems of all sorts. In the last few years, spoken word and poetry slams have taken off in a big way. And not surprisingly so. These venues offer poets a means of disseminating their work to an audience in a world where many literary journals and small presses are folding, and publishing opportunities shrink. MTV, Lollapalooza, and PBS have all taken on the burgeoning world of spoken word and slams, if only for a good year. But in cafés and bars across the country, writers are continuing to gather and read their work. It is one of the more democratic art-making processes, and anyone can participate, if they have the guts.

In 1995, I competed in the San Francisco poetry slams and managed to snag a place on the four-member team that was to go to Ann Arbor to compete in the National Poetry Slams. The last time I had won anything that required some level of brain activity was when I was twelve and placed second in the National Energy Saving Competition.

For the uninitiated, a poetry slam is a competition where the writer has three minutes to read a piece of writing; typically, no props, no costume, and no music are allowed. Then judges, selected from the audience, will score the piece Olympic-style, from zero (some venues allow negative infinity) to ten. The points are tabulated and the highest score wins.

Ann Arbor was a blast. A rookie team, the San Francisco team consisted of Beth, Mario, Russell, and me. We were like the Mod Squad, a multi-culti group (woman, Chinese, Black, gay, straight, Filipino/Latino, white) of writers who were wide-eyed to the world of poetry slams. The Nationals had been going on for some years, and when we arrived in Ann Arbor, we were amazed, shocked, and horrified at how organized the other teams were. Some of the teams had team shirts, laptops with spreadsheet programs to keep tabs on all the competition, timekeepers, routines choreographed down to Exxon-Valdez slick performances, and self-produced tapes, CDs, books, and other merchandise for sale. The San Francisco team, on the other hand, could not even remember where we parked the car or who had the car keys. But we had fun, we read our work, we got good responses, made it to the semifinals and then lost miserably. We drank a lot, smoked a fair amount of pot, flirted with other people, made new friends, and had a shit-load of fun.

The following year, I slammed again and barely made the team that was going to go to Portland, Oregon, for that year's Nationals. The second time around, though, I had begun to see things a little more for what was happening. This time, the bitchy backbiting, scheming, and ego conflicts were clearly evident. They were probably there in Ann Arbor, but then, I was just plain green and had not noticed it to such an extent. Two other teams' time-keepers clocked me at going past the allotted time limit by 0.01 sec and they gleefully lodged a hearty complaint demanding an automatic point deduction. Russell, who was on the team again as well, suffers from a lazy eye and he wears an eye patch to stop his eyeball from rolling about his head. Someone complained that he was wearing a costume and should be immediately disqualified. A poet from another team tried to convince one of our team members that the venue had been changed just minutes before he was to read. And a poet came to me after we scored better than their team, and said, "I just can't believe that that *you* beat us." The slams began to take on the air of high-school debating competitions, but more pathetic because these were grown men and women behaving this way.

For me, the slams were not only about having a lot of fun, but also a political act. In Ann Arbor, I was one of three Asians in a sea of over three hundred competitors. And as far as openly queer work goes, I was again in a serious minority. It was never about winning for me, since I had never really won anything before and don't thrive that well on competition. I had low expectations about my placing and was more concerned about just reading well.

In Portland, we competed our semifinals round at an all-ages venue. I was going to read a piece called "Pisser." The work is about drug addiction, cum-eating and trading sex for comfort, and finding redemption in and from all that. When all those parents and children started coming in, I just knew that the writing was doomed. For a short minute I decided that perhaps I should substitute something less harsh, something funny and sweet, but I decided against it. It was tough, though. In the middle of performing it, this straight couple decided to start making out, and every time a sexual reference came up, the man decided that he was going to laugh loudly in a mocking manner and his girlfriend would then giggle at his manly wit. Later, I found out that the bouncers had to restrain a man who had wanted to charge the stage to hit me.

It is always a challenge doing queer work. You never know whom you will touch, whom you will move, whose lives you will open up to a different reality, and whom you will offend right down to the roots of their existence. When I make that good connection, and I believe that every writer knows when that is happening, it is great. It's what every writer wants. But when I don't, just as "Pisser" did in Portland that night, I know it isn't the quality of my work nor the fact of my life itself, but that homophobia is a very real thing, and sometimes I tend to forget that. More than likely, I choose to ignore it; I refuse to be hindered by a few people's homophobia, racism, prejudice, and narrow-mindedness.

Even before the Nationals in Portland, I had begun to sour on the slam scene somewhat. It wasn't just the competition or the competitiveness of it. But that certainly played its part in my growing distaste. People were starting to take those scores so seriously. Maybe they always did, but I had just started to realize that. I've seen poets weeping outside a venue because "that poem never scored lower than a twenty-six before!" People were just not seeing the irony of the actual act of scoring these works in the first place, as if any poem or poet is or can be 2.4 points better than another and 1.7 points worse than another. Still, it is an ego thing. I must admit that getting high points is such a rush. I've had that rush on many occasions; and getting a low score really does hurt one's ego. That, too, I've experienced on many occasions. But I've always tried to remember that the scoring is all a lark. Of course, some writers do decry the scoring, saying that the idea of assigning a numeric value to writing is gauche and offensive. The maxim, "The point is not the points; The point is poetry!" is chanted ever so often at slams (usually by the ones who are most besotted by the idea of scoring). As a kid, I was always told that it was not whether I win or lose but how I play the game. That made perfect sense, but I still wanted to win because it was the winner who got to bask in all the adoration and glory. But is competition really all that bad? Maybe not, and we do it all the time. When you submit your work to a journal, when you do enter a contest, or when you apply for MFA programs or grants, you are, in effect, competing with others' work. It's just that the competition is not so public, obvious, held up for scrutiny, and fueled by alcohol and/or caffeine.

No, it wasn't the competitiveness, but more the spirit of a lot of the people involved.

Poet Juliette Torrez, a wonderful writer, organizer, and all-around lover of poetry, used to run an e-mail newsletter catering to the slams, where slammers and others vented about rules and such. After the 1997 Nationals, the following was posted by one Rev. Jack Godsey:

> Issue poetry. I know, I know . . . it's hideously uncool to speak out about issue poems. But here are the facts: For one, it's a GIVEN that a "heartfelt," "gut-wrenching" poem about racism (especially if performed by a "minority") or sexism (especially if performed by a woman) will get at least a 9 if not a HIGH 9 by the average judge. Part of this problem is that the VAST majority of judges, especially at the Nationals level, have NOTHING in common with the poets. They are, by and large, white suburban yuppies who think the Slam

is "cool" and "hip" and "relevant" and could care LESS about actual GOOD WRITING. They feel that they SHOULD give these poems such high scores. Now, given, some issue poetry is actually also well-written and personal but those poets are in the minority by a long-shot . . . There is no future in revolutionary poetry . . . There is even LESS future in PERSONAL poetry. I can't think of a single poet at the Regional or National levels that did very well with a poem that was well-written and concerned SOLELY with personal experience untainted by PC pandering. Getting a 25 at the Nationals means absolutely nothing because a 25 is usually the lowest anyone gets. It doesn't matter what your number is; coming in last is still coming in last.

This posting got to the heart of my distaste with the whole scene. I found it interesting that the writer felt that racism, to a minority, and sexism, to a woman, was not a personal thing, and that it was instantly incongruous with "Good Writing." That somehow, racism and sexism when written and spoken by a person of color or woman is a "personal experience" tainted by "PC pandering." That racism and sexism are issues that white suburban yuppies can find nothing relevant in. It does not occur to Godsey, who describes himself as "rental messiah, slam poet, and urban shaman," that the experience of racism and sexism by those most affected by it and their resistance to it, by writing and speaking about it, is an important act. By reducing that act to "PC pandering," Godsey tries to diminish and reduce the severe emotions of pain, anger, and frustration that racism and sexism mark on their victims.

But he is not alone. After a slam in Portland, John Dooley, one of the local poets there, accosted me at an after-slam party, and in his beer-addled stupor said, "The next time, I don't have to do anything, I should just go up to the mike and tell everyone that I'm Chinese and gay and I'll get a good score." Apparently, when you're a colored person, a woman, or queer, you never get good scores because of a good piece of writing, but because of your identities.

At the Nationals, many poets of color were accused of "playing the Race Card." Firstly, it's horrific how the OJ trial has infected our vocabulary with its mindless, unchallenged catchphrases. Secondly, what the hell is the Race Card in the context of slams? Presumably, it's when a person of color talks about race, and when white folks feel bad or guilty or uncomfortable because of it, and a good score is given. Obviously, if the poem, no matter how well written, is scored low, then the Race Card wasn't played, or was played but the white judges (and they usually are) were too smart to fall for it.

We've seen this argument before. From white writers who shriek and holler that they do not get enough publishing and performance opportunities because of multiculturalism, to the argument about how multiculturalism is threatening the Canon of Great Literature, to the continuing battle over the content and curricula of school textbooks in California.

In her infamous *New Yorker* article about "victim art," critic Arlene Croce said that she could not write a proper review about someone she is forced to feel sorry for. Godsey and Croce do have a point, but is empathy such a bad thing? Still, I do know what they refer to. It is disconcerting to see someone go up onstage and read a heart-wrenching poem about being raped or abused, and then turn around after three minutes and demand a score for that. Then there are poets who write persona pieces, where their characters speaking in the work are raped and abused and oppressed, and pass it off as their own experiences.

This commodification of oppression, and the glorification and heroism of oppression, really made me uncomfortable. And it made me question whether I was also guilty of making what Croce has termed "victim art." The effect of persistently hammering the phrase victim art into the psyche of America prompts many people, like Croce and Godsey, to immediately suspect anyone who is a sexual and/or racial minority, who has AIDS, and who is somehow different. This suspicion serves to silence sexual and racial minorities and to make them mistrust and internalize their experiences of oppression.

And in the whole argument of victim art, there is an aspect absent: the victimizer. When Godsey was advocating personal poetry, written from "personal experience untainted by PC pandering," he was in effect calling *for* victim art. But when the writers start talking about the victimizers, that's when he gets all huffy, and it ceases to be art for him, and for many others, too.

At the 1996 Outwrite conference, I participated in my first all-queer slam. Instead of being the fun event that I thought it would be, I was sorely disappointed. The pieces that I witnessed the poets read were heartbreaking: abuse, incest, rape, gay-bashing, racism, failed relationships. *My boyfriend died of AIDS, give me points . . . My girlfriend beat me up, give me points . . .* Patti Smith once said that the artist wears his art instead of his wounds, and I did not want to think that my community was nothing but a pile of wounds. But it seemed that these writers felt that this was the only way to "be good" and "get points." Grief, cruelty, and injustice happen, and writers use these themes to varying degrees of success and with varying degrees of intelligence and sophistication. It is not the wound but how we talk about it and how we dress it. And comfort it. And heal it.

But when you put a work out there, something happens to it. It is no longer the writer scrawling in his or her journal in some smoky café with a latte in hand, or writing in the solitude of an insomniac night. When you publish a piece of writing or perform it publicly, you give up a certain part of it, you do not own its meaning or its emotional control anymore. You want it to find an audience, and that audience will find its own meaning from reading or hearing that work. How they read and understand the piece will depend on so many things that are outside of the writer's control. Some people will look at the work on a purely emotional level and others on a more technical level, and still others will bring their whole life in literature to the table. But that's what the beauty of putting work out there is about. Sure, some readings of the work will be more informed and some readers will be more perceptive, but the audiences will have their way.

There is criticism about reading a work on an emotional level. Critics say that it is not a sophisticated or informed way to look at work. But in the words of Muriel Rukeyser, poetry invites you to feel, to respond, and better than that, poetry invites a total response.

The slams and the spoken-word scene were a way of getting writing out to an audience. It was poetry by ambush, unsuspecting folk would step into a bar for a pint and there was poetry. Some of it may be good and some really bad, but there it was, words upon words. The notion of using the audience to "judge" a work was a nod toward the significance of the audience, and it was an ironic gesture. There was really no real system of awarding points to these works, it was all purely subjective; but that ironic gesture soon got lost in the rabid field of competition.

I always liked the risk of doing queer work to a predominantly straight and white audience, whether they would understand the references or not, and whether they would be comfortable with it or not. There is so much middle-of-the-road work in the slams, so much bland sweetness, and, God! all those poems about poems. Maybe I'm being a little harsh and somewhat bratty here, in the end. It is not a great revelation that different people have different realities that will be written about. We can't all have drug problems and dysfunctional families. But at the same time, because of the judging element and the drive of competition, so often the real work, the true work, and the work that should be read, that needs to be heard, that reflects a fuller spectrum of our individual, our societal, and our communal experiences, is not.

John Berger said that "every authentic poem contributes to the labour of poetry . . . to bring together what life has separated or violence has torn apart. Poetry can repair no loss, but it defies the space which separates. And it does this by its continual labour of reassembling what has been scattered." Continuing Berger's thought, Adrienne Rich writes, "It is not any single poem, or kind of poem, but the coming together of many poems, that can reassemble what has been scattered, can defy the space that separates."

The slams seemed like a real physical coming together of poems. Hundreds of writers from thirty-odd states and even a few from abroad gathered together to read poems and be in each other's company. But competition, conceit, and the drive to win at all costs took over, and every whiff of society's injustices, prejudice, and ignorance was amplified in this setting. I had expected more from people who call themselves writers. But to many of these slammers, being a writer was merely a stepping-stone or a substitute to being a rock star, a celebutant, or some means to gain attention from a world that would otherwise ignore their feeble mettle. Being a writer was reduced to coolness, hipness, and fashion. Maybe history will look back fondly on this artistic movement, and maybe some sense of revisionism will add a veneer of heroism and democracy to it. But for now, the power of poetry has never been more bastardized.

WHAT I DID
LAST SUMMER

Bite Hard, my book of poetry, had finally come out and it was time to whore it. Beth Lisick, who had written the utterly fabbo *Monkey Girl,* published by the same press as I, was going to chuck her workaday routine, climb into her dad's truck (hers got stolen), and go on a mondo road trip, traveling to thirty-odd cities in seven weeks, doing readings and selling books out of the back of her truck. It's like Anne Rice's bus tour but without the bus, the budget, the coffin, or the legions of Goth kids trailing along. I was to accompany her on the southern leg of her tour.

I have had my own preconceived notions about the southern part of the country. Informed by movies and especially TV *(Dukes of Hazzard, BJ and the Bear,* and its spin-off *Lobo),* I expected hillbillies, rednecks, twangy accents, big hair, country music, humorless Christians, and KKK rallies around every corner.

Even before that, weeks before, I had gone to upstate New York to hang out at my friend Ames's little cabin in West Exter, located somewhere near the town of Winfield. I think it's all close to Utica, but I'm not sure. He drove.

California and New York are those states that people have very definite ideas about. Say California, and people immediately think of Hollywood, sunny beaches, cable cars chugging down the Golden Gate Bridge, and *Baywatch*. Truth be told, California is huge, and outside of the bigger cities, the state is a massive sprawling suburb, and then massive sprawling farms, peopled with migrant farm workers.

Say New York, and people think of New York City, maybe *NYPD Blue*, Broadway, and Times Square, even that movie. But here way out along the interstates, New York looks like central California, like the Midwest, like the farm belt. Lots of dairy and cow farms dotting the landscape. If those militant vegetarians want people to stop eating meat, they should just bottle up the smell of those darn cow farms and the gallons of cow poop.

Ames suggested we go to the VFW for their annual Labor Day barbecue. "VFW, are you mad?" I said. "You want me to go to a place filled with veterans, whose proudest, most crowning moment was defending their country from people who look like me, and have possibly killed a whole bunch of people who look like me and might still be possibly having flashbacks?" But the price was right and so we went. The old veterans were cordial and nice, the barbecue was good shit. And the most I got was a lot of stares, some more discreet than others.

Yup, America is white. Recent reports in the media might suggest that the country was being overrun by all these dusky people. Immigrants dashing across the border like the Roadrunner, swimming ashore on rickety boats, and sneaking into airports, stealing all those great garment factory, janitorial, and agricultural jobs that the pure-blooded American high-schoolers all so desperately want and have been training ten years for. And then on *Cops*, it's always the colored folks that are being chased and clobbered. And even on non-"Reality TV" (ha!), the colored folks are still being clobbered by the good cops.

But if you look at the last census report, the country is still 80 percent white, which is a heck of a lot of white, though probably not enough for some folks.

We started our trip in Austin, where I was to meet Beth. She had already been driving all down California through the Southwest and through west Texas.

At the Austin airport I'm whisked off by Hillary, our host and a fellow poet, to do a spot on a local radio show. I'm cautioned about using those seven words, but unfortunately I only know four of those seven words. I read a sweet love poem (no swearing, no fucking), ending it by making some silly comment about how I wished the person it was written for (who had since left) would come to a bitter end.

"Oh no!" Nancy, the radio host with her soothing melted-margarine voice says earnestly. "You must think of love as like a meteorite, that just burns and passes by."

"Yeah, I hope the meteorite will crash into his apartment," I say.

"Oh no!" Nancy and Gayle, her cohost, simultaneously chirp in wide-eyed disapproval. "It's best to move on from a failed relationship," Gayle offers helpfully.

"Now let's hear some music from Namibian bushwomen. I've

always wondered what Namibian bushwomen sound like, haven't you?" Gayle says.

"No, I can't say I know what Namibian bushwomen sound like!" Nancy banters back. Hillary and I leave to the chants of Namibian bushwomen.

We head on to the local bookstore where we are to do an afternoon reading. Two people show up for the reading, one of them had gone to high school with Beth. Beth accidentally smashes the bookstore's little clip-on mike. Austin was spent going to the local swimming hole, a creek that the municipality had dammed up to make a nice cool natural swimming pool, going to clubs and watching bands, drinking loads of beer and enjoying the company, the charms and the hospitality of the locals. In Austin, I discovered the difference between chicken fried steak, chicken fried chicken, and just fried chicken. Chicken fried steak is mainly chicken beaks, feet, and gizzards, shaped into a patty and fried. (Well, it's actually ground beefsteak.) Chicken fried chicken is a moist breast of chicken battered and fried (good eating with ranch dressing). And fried chicken is a hunk of chicken with bone that is battered and fried.

We leave Austin late at night. The roads are less crowded, and the air is less stifling. It is right smack in the middle of summer, and the heat and humidity are unrelenting. The dust from the freeways and the sticky, clammy air we have to drive through are brutal. The plan is to drive until Beth passes out, then we'll look for a cheap motel. Beth has to do all the driving since I don't drive. Not well, at least. She's real cool about it, and I try to pull my weight by reading the maps and navigating. In the cool night air, accompanied by drive-time radio, we pass Waco and Dallas, two places that have made their mark on television sets all over the world. All I know of Dallas is several seasons of the said soap opera. In one early episode, Lucy Ewing, the spoiled niece, is angry at the family. It is her sweet sixteen birthday, and the Ewings are throwing a huge party for her at Southfork. But Jock refuses to allow Lucy to invite her mother, and JR is using the party to make business deals. Lucy is furious and runs off to Waco to look for her mother. Along the way, she is kidnapped by a handsome drifter who robs diners. He makes her sing "Silver Threads and Golden Needles" at a local bar's amateur hour while he robs the place. Then Bobby rescues her. But this was before anyone, except for some ATF agents, knew what was going on in Waco. In the weekday night, Waco is still and quiet and an eerie air hangs over the place. We drive with the windows down and the wind whips through the car with noisy delight. I imagine what it must have been like on the night when the Davidian compound was burnt down, how the air, thick with dark smoke, must have smelled.

Places that we think are chains, like Red Lobster and Sizzler, are actually regional things. Here, they're pretty much the same things but with different unfamiliar names. But it's basically the same fried chicken, the same burgers, the same pizzas, and the same fried seafood joint. We drive past a couple of Hooters, and Beth and I conspire to go there sometime and I will play her retarded charge. Clutching my Human Anatomy coloring book, we'll go in pretending that we think that Hooters is a theme restaurant about owls. "Where are the owls, Aunty Beth?" I'll ask in my Lenny from *Of Mice and Men* on-TNT-movies voice. I imagine that Hooters will have waitresses whose heads turn a little more than 180 degrees as they survey the floor asking, "Who? Who? Who ordered the margarita?" And when we leave, we will buy the Hooters' clip from the gift shop. This is a clip that you use on the back of your

T-shirt so that it will pull your T-shirt snugly over the front of your torso. But of course, we simply end up at Whattaburger.

Next stop: Fayetteville, Arkansas. Along the way, after we cross the Oklahoma border, we stop for lunch at a small, greasy, wood-shack roadside diner. The diner is filled with old men and women, and the old guy sitting in the booth behind us is wearing a faded T-shirt that proudly proclaims "I Am the NRA." There is a pastel airbrushed painting of John Wayne's head hovering over a herd of galloping horses on the wall. I realize what a sight Beth and I must make. She's wearing a halter top, midriff showing, and her hair is an iridescent purple; and I'm tattooed down three-quarters of my arms and so obviously not the chinky from the local Chinese restaurant.

The drive to Fayetteville is scenic, a lot of mountains and crafts shops. We keep thinking we should stop for googly-eyed almond tabletop knickknacks as souvenirs but keep our urges in check and drive on. We drive past a nuclear reactor and it looks like it does in movies: two cylindrical concrete top hats surrounded by a huge pond, ominously lurking over the lush green countryside. One of the tourist attractions of the Ozarks is the Jesus of the Ozarks. Some zealous Christians decided that they wanted to build a statue of Jesus to rival the one in Rio de Janeiro. What better way to show their love for our Lord and Savior than by erecting an epic Jesus, arms outstretched to receive his flock? Only problem was that they had originally built it too high and had to cut the poor Lord off at the knees, so the Jesus of the Ozarks looks like a stumpy midget Christ. And he has a red light on the top of his holy head to warn planes of his blessings.

In Fayetteville, I'm sitting by the bar at the club we are about to read at. The locals are all excited, and the local poetry slam team are out to help bring in an audience for us. I'm sitting at the bar nursing my beer and going over what I will read. It's always tough to know how much queer an audience can take. Should I do the cocksucker piece? the fist-fucking piece? A tall thin handsome grizzled man comes up to me. "Are you Justin?" he asks, and I tell him that I am. "This is for you," he says, and gives me a small bunch of wildflowers and a card, inside which is written: *The queer and faerie communities welcome you to the Ozarks.* Yes, I think I will read the cocksucking and fist-fucking pieces tonight!

We meet up with Brenda, a local writer, whose day job is home-care provider. She takes care of AIDS patients in Fayetteville. When she talks about her work, it surprises me at first. After close to twenty years of the AIDS epidemic, and the constant reminders that AIDS is not merely a disease in the big cities, and all that, it still takes me by surprise when I realize that there are untold numbers of people who are living in this country who have AIDS but do not have the ready and overwhelming access to drugs, services, information, and a community as we do in San Francisco or New York. They've traded all that for home, or what they know as home. That people actually do "go home to die," and that families do take care of their sick children, and old friends do care.

Our next day in Fayetteville, our host Lisa takes us shooting in Hogeye with her boyfriend, who may or may not have ties to the Ozarks militia. We nip into the gun shop to buy bullets, and I am amazed how cheap bullets are, a mere fiver for a box of thirty-six, such a deal. The gun shop is also a pawnshop and they have a dazzling display of pro-NRA, anti-Clinton bumper stickers. We drive up to Lisa's boyfriend's cabin. His family has lived on the mountain for the last five or so generations. It's like the Waltons but with lots of guns. Greg has saddled up the horses for us and we ride up to the top of the mountain to shoot up tree stumps. Greg has broken out his cache of cop-killer bullets, the ones with the armor-piercing inner core for us to use. We protest—since these bullets are now illegal, we don't want him to waste it on us greenhorns. But he graciously lets us shoot them. We start with a nice Magnum, firing it into a cross section of a felled tree.

I was so Kelly Garrett. I had never held a real gun before, much less fired one, but amazingly I hit all my targets that day. The first blast from the gun was incredible: the ringing in my ears, the ricochet jerking my arm back. Beth and I were amazed that we knew how to ride horses and shoot guns just from watching TV. All those episodes of *Dynasty* when Krystle went riding on Allegria at Delta Rho Farms sure helped. After firing off the Magnum, we head back down to the cabin to fire off Chinese-made AK-47s and shotguns. The AK-47s were great. "The gun that won the Vietnam War!" Greg tells us, as he shows us how to attach the massive bayonet to the tip of the gun and how to thrust it into someone's stomach. It's very Rambo. The AK-47s are semiautomatic things that just crack and spew bullets all over the place, no kickback, no fuss, easy as turning on the faucet. It's the postal worker's wet dream. You can't have a clip that contains more than thirty bullets, but Greg shows us how to duct-tape another clip to the existing one so that you can change the clip in a blink. Later, back in the car and on the road again with Beth, I confess that the Vietnam War comment had me really uncomfortable. After all, who was the gook in this whole show-and-tell here? "I just bit my tongue and didn't say anything," I said.

"He didn't say that we won the war, he said it was the *gun* that won the war, and I guess maybe the Vietcong had the Chinese-made guns," Beth offers.

The shotguns proved to be more of a challenge. Still, Beth and I knew how to reload the shotgun from watching Linda Hamilton in *Terminator 2*. Damn, I was butch. We fired off the shotguns at paper plates and again, I hit all my targets. Beth was having a more difficult time. "Try to relax," Greg advises. "You seem so tense."

"Maybe it's because I have a huge gun in my hands," Beth replies. Still, in a bikini and with that gun, she would be any militia guy's choice pinup for all the long months holed up in his mountain cabin waiting for the ATF raid.

Shooting guns is quite addictive and the power of it is undeniable: Once the bullet leaves the barrel, it will go its way in split seconds and there is nothing to stop it.

Beth and I leave Fayetteville and drive through the Ozarks. Next stop: Memphis.

You cannot go to Memphis and not go to Graceland. Like most monumental buildings, Graceland is smaller than I expect. The plaza is across from the mansion and we dutifully buy our tickets. We're only going to do the house tour, skipping the garage and plane tour both of which will cost extra. Graceland is filled with older doughy white-trash tourists, and young Japanese tourists, the ones who are endlessly enamored of Americana and will buy all those Confederate flags and decorate with them without really understanding what they mean. In line to board the bus that will take us across the street to Graceland proper, we spy an older woman who's wearing a tank top so she can flaunt the young Elvis postage stamp tattoo on her free-flabbing sausage arms.

We get out the headsets for the audio tour of the mansion and we are off. Beth and I are terrified that we might actually say something that may be perceived to be irreverent and get beat up by the devotees and kicked out of Graceland. The tour starts with the living room and the dining room. Everything is cheesy sixties and seventies over-the-top metallic art deco meets rococoan psychedelia psychodrama. The tour proceeds through the kitchen and into the rec room. It's gorgeous. The room is done up in yards upon yards of pleated batik fabric from floor to ceiling. We go to the Jungle Room, famous for its green-shag carpeting among other things. Elvis used to record in this room, and apparently the shag helps the acoustics. In spite of a segment on *House of Style*, I never knew how to use shag carpeting on the walls until now. I am disappointed that we are not allowed onto the second floor. I so much wanted to see the bedrooms and the bathrooms (what kinds of toiletries? what kind of loo rolls?). Then it's off to the offices, the stables (converted into museum), and the annex where all the gold records, awards, and costumes are housed. Elvis was quite enamored of law enforcement and had even offered to spy for the FBI. A nice note from J. Edgar Hoover politely turning down his offer is framed and hung on the wall. Elvis was also quite taken by Eastern mysticism, martial arts, and religions. His nunchaks and ninja paraphernalia are displayed. Another surprise since Elvis is always represented as the ultimate all-American icon, worshiping God and country, and recording albums full of hymns. In fact, all his Grammys (on display too) were for his gospel recordings. Elvis's costumes are also displayed. I had only seen them on the man himself, as he sashayed across the TV screens, on video, and in countless photographs. But here, they were tacked to the wall like mounted butterflies. It all just seems so unreal.

The audio tour is also terribly reverent to the King. Sample: "Soon, life on the road took its toll. Elvis developed health problems . . ." "He and Priscilla separated, but they still remained loving parents to little Lisa Marie . . ." and "That was the last concert

Elvis gave. Later that afternoon, he passed away." All of these translates to: He took loads of drugs and got fat, he didn't want to fuck Priscilla after she dropped the bun, and he had a heart attack while trying to squeeze out a U-Blocker on the loo.

The tour ends at the Eternal Flame, where the graves of Elvis and his parents are. People are weeping and taking photos. Devotees leave flowers, cards, teddy bears, and little mementos which the estate assures will be either saved for the archives or sent to children's hospitals.

Then it's back to Graceland the mall to buy postcards, fridge magnets, and all sorts of Elvis-related stuff. I send my mom some little souvenirs. She is a big Elvis fan, and family stories have it that her father actually tossed her Elvis record out of the window when she first played it in the house.

The reading in Memphis goes well. We read at the P&H Cafe, which is run by Wanda, a boisterous Janis Joplin-esque lady who wears big hats and sasses everyone. In Memphis, too, we partake of our first taste of Memphis pork sandwiches. By this time, my affinity toward pork is well evident, and I'm trying to keep my servings of pork down to six a week. It's difficult but I try.

We leave Memphis and drive through Mississippi, stopping at a small motel in the wee hours of the morning. A lot of the small motels are independently owned and operated by South Asians, we find. The next morning, we drive into Birmingham, Alabama, and we stop in the city center to look at the sculpture garden. A small walkway around the park takes us from one huge brass sculpture to another depicting the civil-rights struggle. In the summer, there's a water hose actually spraying a sculpture of civil-rights protesters. One of the most terrifying sculptures is of police dogs attacking two little Black children. The detail captured in the brass is amazing, and the looks on the children's faces and the ferocity of the dogs are powerful.

Standing in that park on that summer afternoon, I feel the weight of history. That on that very soil, thirty some years ago, all this heroism, passion, anger, courage, and fear came head to head with hatred and intolerance. A few months later, I will find myself in Dallas at the Texas School Book Depository and wandering around Dealey Plaza, and I will feel that same sense of weight. I wonder if younger queer kids will one day look at streets where ACT UP and Queer Nation protested during those Reagan-Bush years and feel that same weight.

Throughout our road trip, I keep looking out for other Asians, and apart from the South Asians we rent the motel rooms from and later in Atlanta, I hardly see any on the streets. The only sign of anyone Asian comes from the Chinese restaurants that we pass. They are all named nonthreateningly and catering to that sense of Western orientalia: Golden Wok, House of Won Ton, Potsticker Palace, China House "Home of the $4.99 Buffet," The Fortune Cookie, and Chop Suey Palace.

After much driving, we make it to our destination: Athens, Georgia. Athens was one of those magical places of college rock that existed in my mind. In Athens, we are going to stay with Marie, an older Southern socialite, who is a friend of a friend of Beth's. She is beautiful, gracious, and utterly charming. And her house is amazingly beautiful. It was built in the 1850s and a new annex was added on in the 1890s to bring the kitchen indoors. The floors are interlaced with oak and maple hardwoods so that they are striated, and the place is beautifully decorated with antique furniture. We sleep in four-poster beds with good linen and well-padded mattresses, such a change from crashing on people's couches and sleeping in cheap, dinky motels. Usually, Beth and I give our hosts our books as a token of our appreciation for putting us up, but this time, we're afraid that our books might sully this beautiful house.

I had no real idea what to expect Athens to be like. Maybe I thought it was going to be a little more rock and roll. But really, it's just another college town with great herds of college kids doing what they do: partying, chugging beer, and shagging.

The reading in Athens was organized by Doug, a local poet, and he comes with us when we depart for Asheville, North Carolina, the next day. We stop at a Cracker Barrel, which is another magical place to me because in the late eighties, during the heydays of Queer Nation, the Southern and Midwestern chapters of QN had done an action against Cracker Barrel for firing a gay waiter. Cracker Barrel is a restaurant and Southern gift shop—i.e., homey tchotchkas with that suburban country kitchen feel, pastel rabbits and ducks, dried vegetation, and aprons and dish towels that either tell a story or have an elaborate recipe for some kind of pie. Their pork chops are great.

In South Carolina, half the billboards are of a Christian nature. Church battling against church for the souls and offerings of the believers. "Oh look, that's so sweet," Beth says as she spies some headstones on someone's front lawn. Until we drive closer, then we see that the headstones do not commemorate the family's dearly departed. Instead, they proclaim ABORTION KILLS in bright red letters. Later we will see trucks that have these headstones mounted on their beds.

We get into Asheville, which is supposed to be a liberal bastion of this part of the country. Whatever. Our hosts put us up at the local boardinghouse; apparently, the only boardinghouse. Beth and Doug end up in the girls' room since the boys' room is all full. At the reading later that night, we feel kind of weird that everyone seems to read their work as if it were Shakespeare-in-the-Bar. We seem so common and uncouth with our regular voices.

We nip back to Athens the next day, where we go our separate ways; Beth continues on to New York, and I hop on a bus to go to Atlanta. I've decided to stay at a youth hostel. Maybe I'm getting older, but it's getting harder for me to stay at youth hostels. The beds really hurt, and my bones and muscles ache like fuck. But there's something to be said for sleeping in a room with five other strange men, all in our underwear. Maybe it's me but I keep thinking that someone is masturbating and that I should be awake for it. I do not get much sleep.

In Atlanta, I end up at the CNN Studio tour seeing how they schlep their twenty-four-hour news show together. The tour guides look ragged, and they must be, having to schlep groups every other hour through the building, and saying the same vaguely informative lines and punch lines over and over again. But that's the nature of CNN. The same news programs and the same news reports repeat endlessly through the day. I especially love how the tour guides refer to their boss as "Ted" (e.g., "Oh no, Ted doesn't want to acquire any more satellites."), as if they personally knew Ted Turner, and as if he sat to lunch with them weekly to tell them his plans.

The news anchors—those bastions of hair, makeup, truth, and reliability, that creep into our televisions nightly, or rather every single damn minute of the day in CNN's case—look really odd. Because of the studio lighting, they have to pile on that makeup, and in the absence of the television screen, they just look so phony. Typically, I would never trust anyone with so much makeup on their faces that they look like waxworks. There was supposed to be a Chinese-speaking tour, but because of the lack of Chinese-speaking tourists, the guides have dumped a Chinese family with this group without the aid of any translation. The poor family look lost and bored but like the newsmaking they're witnessing; the guides simply just don't care. The tour ends, where else, but in the gift shop, where you can buy all sorts of Ted Turner cable-station products: from Wrestlemania and NWO wrestling souvenirs to TNT movie memorabilia. Or you can get photos of yourself taken with a cardboard cutout of a CNN anchor.

Then it's off to the World of Coca-Cola, a three-story building that is essentially an advertisement for Coke. I've always liked Coke, it has been my preferred soft drink since I was a wee lad. The World of Coca-Cola shows us how Coke was invented and marketed from its beginnings all the way up to now. The best part of the tour was watching all those Coca-Cola TV ads from the 1970s to the present. I distinctly remember how we always looked forward to them when they came on the television, because they were just so catchy and fun and well made. Before you leave the building, there is a room of soda fountains where you can sample Coca-Cola products from around the world. It's amazing how some Americans have never heard of, seen, or tasted a lychee before. By the end of the World of Coca-Cola experience, I never wanted a diet Pepsi more in my life.

I was fine throughout all of the South, but in Atlanta, suddenly the accents started to get to me and I just could not understand what the fuck a lot of people were saying. At the food court, I couldn't figure out if the guy at the Captain Cajun was speaking with an accent or if he was trying to speak Chinese to me.

Eventually, I make it home to San Francisco, home with all the freaks and weirdos and multi-culti pockets that make me love this city so much. Like all road trips, there is always a sense of leaving something of oneself and coming back with a heightened sense of it. I am glad I made this trip. Sometimes, we let our fear of the unknown and our preconceptions of a place prevent us from going where we please. When I told people I was going to do this trip, more than a few were shocked and asked why I was going. Wasn't I afraid of the racism and the potential for trouble? I, too, had a smudge of this fear, but as I traveled through the South, crossing state line after state line, and in and out of hundreds of cities where hundreds and thousands of people live and work, that apprehension faded quickly. Committing sodomy across four state lines did help make the trip a little more fun, too.

There are millions of lives out there, and each of them comes with its own stories and circumstances. I often hear reports of incidents of racism, homophobia, and gay-bashing in these areas, and I do not doubt that they do happen. But these also happen in the big cities. Perhaps we want to believe that the other, the people who live on the other side of the tracks, are more uncouth and less civil than we are, that they are capable of worse things.

If anything, this trip gave me a sense of connectedness with the country that I had never felt before. In some strange way, because of the way people opened themselves to us, I felt that I could belong to any part of this country. That I had a right to be there, and others would see that, too. That things weren't really all that different, just moving at a different speed. And I had never felt more American than at this time.

DON'T ASK ISADORA, ASK ME!

I am a twenty-seven-year-old man and I have a girl-friend. We have a good sex life but lately, I've been noticing this guy in the office. He works in the mail room and I find myself very attracted to him and I constantly find myself fantasizing about having sex with him. Should I tell my girlfriend? Should I approach this guy? I'm not even sure he's gay or that I am? What should I do?

You are not gay. You are just a straight man who likes to have sex with men. Rest assured that there are many men like you. You might want to seek them out at truck stops on I-80 or in the financial district to form a support group. By all means, tell your girlfriend. Remember to describe every gory detail about how you want to scrape the shit out of your hunka-hunka fantasy man's asshole with your tongue. If she's not supportive of your fantasies, then she probably doesn't really love you. Your next step is to boldly approach this fantasy man. You must take control of your desires. He is probably gay because gay men tend to give out subconscious signals to the rest of the world that they are gay. This is called gaydar. Invent excuses to go to the mail room, especially after work hours, invite him to the gym, or to go to the office rest room and then make your move. Tell him what you want and more than likely he'll respond positively, unless, of course, you are a butt-fucking troll. But with your girlfriend and your fantasy man, always remember, communication is the key.

———

I notice that after my boyfriend ejaculates on me, I get itchy where his cum has been on my skin. Am I allergic to his semen?

Yes. You are allergic to his semen. If he loves you, he will only ejaculate when you are out of the room, preferably when you are at work. But there are other options, too. You could have sex with your clothes on, and he can come on you when you are fully clothed. If you love him, this should not be a problem. You need not wear your good clothes. You could just go to some thrift store and buy clothes, preferably parkas, ponchos, and knitted bodysuits, for sex. And remember, communication is the key.

———

My boyfriend and I are very close and have a great sex life. However, there is one problem: After we've made love he just wants to roll over and go to sleep, while I want to cuddle and kiss. Does this mean he's just using me?

Me, me, me. Is that all you ever think of? Yourself? Well, the whole world just revolves around your fleshy butt, doesn't it? Isn't it enough that someone has taken the time out to poke you? All you can think is more more more, mememe. But who am I to judge; I am here to help your problems no matter how inane. You can solve this problem in a number of ways. You might try going ahead and cuddling and kissing him while he is asleep. If that is not satisfying, try letting him sleep for a few minutes then wake him up and demand snuggling. If that doesn't work, go to the kitchen and get a big knife, sit beside him on the bed, and wait till he wakes up (you may also wake him up yourself but the effect is not the same). When he opens his eyes, brandish the knife, and shriek, "Would you like some pecan pie?" but slur and mumble the sentence so that it sounds like "Snuggle or die!" But oh hell, I can't lie to you anymore: He probably did use you, you slut. You two can overcome this by communicating. After all, communication is the key.

———

The other day, my best friend told me about his secret fetish. He likes to entertain and he will invite a few friends over for dinner and in the course of preparing the meal, he will masturbate and ejaculate into the

sauce. He likes to watch the unsuspecting guests eat his semen. I told him this was gross. But now, after the last party, one of his guests has become ill. Could his semen have anything to do with it?

Again, I must stress, communication is the key. You might want to buy my new book and tape, *Communication Is the Key: 15 Simple Lessons on Communicating* ($24.95), to start with. It is unlikely that your friend's sick and twisted habit caused the illness considering the others seemed to be okay. However, ejaculating in sauces is not to be advised. Very often semen can cause the sauce to curdle up and turn. Ejaculate only on a low heat or on a simmer. If you are unsure, you should remove the pan from the fire before ejaculating. Also, be warned: Semen can react quite adversely with some spices such as dill and tarragon, and in some cases can turn these spices quite bitter. Also, chilies will bind to the little spermies and spot the sauce, making it hotter and less controllable (the sauce not the sperm). Never serve semen with any fish or seafood. It is best kept to poultry.

———

I have a brother who is gay. He doesn't know that I know, that pretty much everyone knows it, even members of our family. I guess he just doesn't want to confront me with what he is. Should I tell him I know, or should I wait until he tells me?

Are you sure your brother is gay? He could merely be an effeminate straight man, or a straight man with gay characteristics like the propensity to suck cock and get fucked in the butt by hairy fat men. Once you are sure that your brother is gay, you should confront him with it. Pick a huge family gathering: Thanksgiving, Christmas, wedding, or a big dinner are best. You want to spare him the embarrassment of having to admit to the family separately, so having him admit to everybody at once is best. During dinner, drop hints that you know: Point the turkey or chicken's ass at him and use the carving knife to diddle it in his face. Offer him a wine cooler. Talk about things that gay people enjoy, like celebrity gossip and home decorating. Then choose the right moment and say, "Alright! Everyone who's gay raise your hands!" Everyone will look at him and he'll know that everyone knows. Say supportive things like: "If I were male and not related to you, I'd suck your cock, too." Or "You have a cute butt, do you do any special exercises to keep it in shape?" It is so important that you communicate because communication is the key.

———

AFTER YOKO

FAGGOT PIECE

Listen to remixed house music
on your headphones
for ten hours straight
Thinking of nothing
but Bob & Rod Jackson-Paris.
Piece ends when you finish
your prescription of antidepressants.

j.c. 1995 spring

PIECE OF SHIT PIECE

Get your lover to crap on the mat.
Sniff at the piece of shit
as if it were your lover.
Bite the piece of shit
i. with love and tenderness.
ii. with anguish and despair.
iii. with ambition.

j.c. 1995 spring

FAG PIECE

Buy as many rainbow-motifed
objects as you can afford.
Shove them up your ass one by one.
Challenge your friends to a competition
seeing who can shove more up the ass.

j.c. 1994 summer

DEAD FAG PIECE

(unrealized film script)
Ask the audience to
1. not touch anyone who knows someone who's dead.
2. imagine their favorite gay icon murdering them.

j.c. 1994 winter

ATTACK OF THE WHITE BUDDHISTS

Can you not flick the shit out of your fingernail these days and not have it hit one of those damn White Buddhists right in the lotus?

Just a few years ago, it seemed like they were all Hindu, buying up all the sitar music at Streetlight, and taking cooking lessons at the Bombay Culinary Institute in Sunnyvale. The lucky ones who dared venture to Chinatown to the cheap cheap travel agents managed to find a good ticket, dashing off to India for a good deal of Indiany stuff, swimming in the holy Ganges and coming home with parasites swimming in their blood, which I'm sure many mistook for some kind of divine blessing of enlightenment. Until the harsh reality of blood in the stools took over.

But now, nothing beats the calm, centered, self-actualization of the Buddhist Thing.

I met my first White Buddhist in Hawaii. Dr. Bob was a medical doctor, but he really just wanted to be a professional Buddhist. He came from oodles of money and he picked me up one day at Ala Moana Beach Park. He offered me a room in his house, and, at that time, I was living in this horrid situation with this strange Australian guy who kept wanting to oof me and I would have done it if his damn dick didn't look like an asparagus spear. (Up until then I had only eaten canned asparagus, and even then, the fresh variety didn't thrill me too much, but we're not talking about vegetables.) So I moved into Dr. Bob's multilevel house in the Manoa Valley. His house had a steam room and a huge garden made to look like a tropical rain forest complete with guest room built into a huge tree. It sure beat living in the dorms. When I came into the living situation, Dr. Bob had just sponsored a seventeen-year-old Chinese student from Beijing and made the poor boy sleep with him every other day. A year later, the boy married his forty-eight-year-old English tutor, and they ran off to live somewhere in Arizona. Dr. Bob ran a child adoption agency out of his home, and many years later, I found out that he was arrested and prosecuted for selling black-market Third World babies, but his daddy, some high-ranking colonel in the army—and you know the army owns half of Hawaii—got him off. All this from a guy who led the whole household in daily meditation sessions and then . . . hot-tubbing!

Selling dusky babies to really liberal couples in the Midwest is not a typical White Buddhist trait. But there's something about this whole Tibetan Buddhist thing that's become so chic lately that it's just not right.

Every time you peek into *People* magazine, the Dalai Lama is being photographed with Cindy and Naomi and Claudia at the Fashion Cafe. And look, here's a picture of Big Master D presenting Goldie Hawn with her own special mantra. And look, here's Sharon Stone kissing Big Master D, who's kissing Richard Gere. Next, he and Natalie Cole will be presenting Best New Artist at the Grammys, then it's off to the Academy Awards to present Best Cinematography with Keanu.

Over here in India, Steven Seagal, star of *Hard To Kill, Under Siege I* and *II, Above The Law,* and the ecological epic *Fire Down Below* (where he saves the Eskimos from the evil oil barons), was designated as the conscious reincarnation of a lama by the supreme head of a Tibetan Buddhist sect. To celebrate his newfound spiritual rebirth, he makes *The Glimmer Man,* playing a cop who solves crimes with Buddhist skills and martial arts, instead of guns.

Welcome to Lamapalooza.

And on the sidestage, a Buddhist nun is telling of the torture and rape she endured at the hands of Chinese prison guards while this chick, decked out in her X-Girl/Stüssy/Diesel wear, is making out with her boyfriend. Next week, Lilith Fair!

And on the main stage, all the spotty teenagers and twentysomethings are crushing forward to get to the stage, chanting "Beastie Boys" (1996) or "Smashing Pumpkins" (1997), while a Buddhist monk retells his experiences of imprisonment and torture; he closes his eyes and speaks haltingly in broken English, trying to explain what it's like to have a cattle prod stuck down his throat for his beliefs, while the kids are restless for some cool breakbeats or the jangly guitar sounds of James Iha. "Oh, why don't they speak English?" this punked-out dude fumes. "Honey, do you have any more Diet Coke in your bag?" his girlfriend whines. "Did Lester take all the pot again, he's such an asshole. That's the last Tibetan Freedom Concert we ever go to with him!"

Later, these kids will wear their souvenir T-shirts and redecorate their rooms in Tibetan Buddhisty motifs. When they grow older and into their yuppie corporate jobs, they'll be able to buy the real Tibetty stuff from those quaint shops on Union Street. They can trot over to the SuperCrown to buy all the Buddhisty books for under three dollars, under five dollars, under ten dollars, and, just for Christmas, under fifteen dollars. Just so that they'll have some context when they do see *Seven Years in Tibet* on laser disc again, and when they go to that lecture at the Shambala Institute by yet another crusty older White Buddhist, who actually *did* go to an actual authentic for real Tibetan monastery for seven years.

I have this vision: somewhere in Tibet, there are all these Tibetans who are Christians. They have prayer meetings and Bible study, they translate Jack Chick pamphlets into Tibetan and distribute them at the marketplace. They redecorate their homes with pictures of the crucifixion of Jesus. A picture of Jesus in the Garden of Gethsemane hangs in the kitchen. One of the lucky Buddhists has the actual prayer vestments of Billy Graham framed and hung in a place of honor in his living room. "Setovan! Tell us again how you got his holiness the Reverend Graham's prayer robes!" his friends beg. Seto ("Chuck" to his friends) sighs, but secretly he's glad to be able to retell of how he meet Billy Graham at his 1982 "I've Found It" prayer rally and evangelical mission at Dodger Stadium. Every week, they gather together to have Bible study and to read daily devotions from Corrie Ten Boom's *Daily Meditations*; they take courage from Corrie's testimonies of hiding from the Nazis and her subsequent internment in the death camps at Auschwitz. They have potlucks and sing modern jazzed-up versions of hymns like "What a Friend We Have in Jesus," "Holy Holy Holy," and "Abba Father We Adore Thee." And they all really really like LeAnn Rimes.

Right now, all these White Buddhists will be thinking that I probably need a little dose of Buddhist teachings to quell my cynicism. I really have nothing against Buddhism at all, it's just that these damn White Buddhists take it all so seriously, and make such a damn production out of it all. Diseases, poverty, exploitation of the poor, ethnic violence and strife are still a part of life in so many Asian nations. There is still so much violence and bigotry directed toward Asians in America, and there is a backlash against immigrants in the United States (the Asian, Middle Eastern, Mexican, and South American ones at least; I mean, does anyone ever question how all those European ice skaters get into this country?). Congress keeps passing more restrictive immigration-reform laws. And so many Asians in America and abroad are wage slaves, sloughing with the jingle of US dollars and Big Macs in their eyes. But you wouldn't know it the way these White Buddhists run over each other to kiss the Dalai Lama or any and every other lama's yellow, fungus-encrusted toenails. As long as they have happy Tibetans to bless their Lexus and Amex conscience, fuck the rest of those dusky people.

So go on. Buy your mantras and meditate until your bottom falls out. Buy your Buddhisty products and redecorate. Spend your seven years in Shangri-La, mosh for the freedom of a nation, learn history from the cineplex, do the mandala hustle-cha-cha with your version of Kerouac and Ginsberg. Feel like you've cornered the market on peace and harmony no matter how you act or behave. Keep telling yourself you're a better person because of it.

I just want to baste the pot roast in your vegetarian blood.

DOWNLOADS (A SCRIPT FOR A DOCUMENTARY)

INTRO

4-to-5-(perhaps less) second montage of quick flashes of Consent
screens (approx. 12 to 15 screens)
(sudden black)

(beat)

PART ONE

(carnival Muzak)

(old time carnival barker's voice)

Ladies and Gentlemen. Welcome to alt dot sex dot the whole-wide-world-wide-web-wide-world.

See! Live human sex acts. See! Chicks with dicks. Dicks with chicks. Leather-Rubber-Plastic-Feathered-Polyester Sex Fetish Acts. Shit-eating. Piss-drinking. Big hooters, nanas, and bazongas. Gigantic asses. Jumbo ball sacs. Testicles like you've-never-seen-before. Pierced dicks, pierced clits, got them all. Dirty boys and girls with even dirtier minds. Boy sex, girl sex, het sex, fat sex. Teenage whores and slutty jocks. Porn stars, movie stars, TV stars, music stars, superstars from the 50s 60s 70s 80s and 90s. Tarts, tramps, and whores. Blow jobs, snow jobs, toe jobs, rim jobs, nose jobs, fist jobs, odd jobs, and joe bobs. Muff-diving, bush-wacking, clit-bumping, dick-wanking, hole-licking; everything can and will be sucked. Asphyxiation, polymorphxiation, fuckerifphyxiation. Sex with all forms of beasts, quadruped, biped, triped, polyped, reptile, mammal, vertebrate and invertebrate. Sex with dildos, Coke bottles, canned fruit, stuffed animals, and, yes, even sex with Barbie dolls and other inanimate objects. Dicks, dongs, cocks, wing-dings, cunts, twats, tits, nips, armpits. Crotches, tuckboxes, baskets, pubic mounts. And yes, even just plain old fucking. Yes, even one-on-one boy-boy boy-girl girl-girl fucking.

See! Men expose their wives and girlfriends for all to see.

See! Men expose themselves for all the world to see.

See! Couples, three-ways, four-ways, five-ways, and every which way possible.

See! Cum-covered body parts and bodily fluids used in ways Never Imagined By Nature.

See! (Virtually) Live Triple-X sex acts, in the Smuttiest Show in the Whole-wide-world-wide-web-wide-world!

PART TWO: WAITING

Waiting. In the world of cybersmut, foreplay is reduced to minutes. Digits on the screen tell you how much longer before the promise of smut, porn, sex, and titillation is delivered right in bits and bytes, pixels and shades, right into your lap. It's not picture perfect, not the stuff of glossy sheen found in magazines, but it's here, it's now, it's a seemingly endless well of dirt, filth, perversion. Every proclivity is available, no matter how strange, twisted, bewildering, or unmentionable. It's all there for your pleasure.

Whether you're downloading in private (the electronic equivalent of masturbating), with a partner, or in a group, a stag party, a gangbang of cyberwotzits, there is the promise of curing what ails you, what will get you off, what will perk your hormones, satisfy your need for oomph and grind.

Things to do while your waiting for your smut to download:

1. Masturbate in anticipation.
2. Clip your toenails.

3. Rearrange your bookshelf.
4. Feed the cat or dog.
5. Read porn magazines.

PART THREE: PAYLOAD

You get your file downloaded. It's sitting on your desktop. It's labeled rather enticingly: "dk10inch," "sluthole," "fuckface," etc. You want your porn bad, you want to see, you want your taste of perversion, your fix of groin smack. Unfortunately, file #1 has been decoded in a manner that neither you nor your computer is able to decipher, file #2 was uploaded improperly and chunks of it are missing, file #3 was corrupted, file #4 was incompatible, file #5 was labeled far too suggestively for its mild contents, and file #6 was labeled dishonestly and was nothing like its namesake but merely an advertisement for long-distance savings.

Back to the pool to look for more. It's like bobbing for the forbidden apple in the Garden of Eden. You have all the time in the world, you just don't have all the hardware and software that would comfort your dick in this silicon world.

PART FOUR: WOW

It's not all that bad, really. There is some priceless stuff. Best of all, when done right, it's instant smut. Ovaltine Folgers smut: right there, right now, no hassles. Some really blow-yer-balls-off pictures of amateurs, real people, professionals that qualify as porn, the stuff that pushes all the right buttons so firmly.

And beyond porn stars and the regular generic buffed notions of sexuality, the whole wide world of sexuality opens up like Ali Baba's cave. Coming out in terms of one's sexual proclivities is easier as on-line virtual communities are suddenly created. The few, the certain, and the kinky find themselves not so alone. Someone needs to share his desire to shit in diapers, to be a baby, to get splodged, to get asphyxiated. Someone out there needs to share his desire for amputees, midgets, animals, and hairy chicks and dudes.

PART FIVE: WON'T SOMEBODY THINK OF THE CHILDREN!

The current discourse on the Internet and porn has focused largely on young people's access to pornographic images. Some people say that the Internet should be censored, that some level of responsibility and control needs to be in place. Some people say that parents should take more responsibility in what their children do on the computers.

Kids have always been and will always be interested in human sexuality. It's all part of growing up. Some kids will learn from their parents, elders, and teachers, some will learn from the schoolyard and their friends, and some will simply figure it out. They will be curious about the body, about bodies. Kids used to try to sneak porn magazines, and they're still doing it, this time on an electronic level. Both methods are not that easy. The latter requires much hardware and software and a certain degree of knowledge of computer gizmotry. And if both methods should fail, there's always the videostore, TV, the movies, Mom and Dad's stash, or the trusty schoolyard. Sex education and communication by educators, parents, and guardians about sexuality will help. But who's got all the time in the world these days? And who really wants to talk about all that embarrassing sex stuff? Only the people on MTV's *Loveline.*

PART SIX: SCARY STUFF 1

Nothing is all good or all bad, or at least very few things are all good or all bad. The technology is neither good nor bad. Porn may be morally or politically good or bad depending on whom you ask. The spectrum swings wide with variables in the production of the images and the differences in opinions and politics.

The discourse on the Internet and porn has also focused very specifically on child pornography. Child pornography is a very repellent and odious thing. Still, much of the hysteria on the issue seems to occur in a certain sphere of paranoia and uncertainty. Often, the pictures found in what are perceived to be child porn sites and groups are merely model catalogues and advertisements. Someone has taken the JC Penney and Sears catalogues and scanned the youngsters' pictures and relabeled the image to be something pornographic. The youngsters are usually not naked and the recontextualization of the images is disturbing. Those same catalogues are sent to every household with a mail slot. When did those images metamorphosize from megastore advertisement selling T-shirts and culottes to one of the lowest forms of pornography, to wank-off material? When did Macauley Caulkin's bathroom scene in *Home Alone* become pornography?

Currently, it is illegal to obtain child pornography and to make a fake child-porn photograph on the Internet by scanning different parts of pictures to make a composite kiddie-porn image. Of course, there are real pictures of obviously underage youths in various stages of undress and nudity. A lot of pictures are from nudist magazines. It is difficult to look at these pictures. There is a strange sense of guilt, shame, and fear attached to seeing these pictures, yet there is also a voyeuristic quality to it. You hear so much about them so you want to see what the fuss is about. And when that image appears on the screen, it's far too late to look away.

PART SEVEN: SCARY STUFF 2

Very much absent in the debate about porn on the Internet is the issue of race. Yup, good ol' America finds a way to commodify race and sexuality into neat little groups and sites. The big threatening Black dick and the invading Latino dick get special attention. Black Mama and hot Latina babes shake their groove things for you. Asians are represented by pussies and oriental sluts ready to suck Yankee dick (so we're led to believe.) Asian men are rarely seen. We've been in this territory before. Still, one gets the idea that most of the porn is made for white consumption. Many of the sites are of white meat. Asian ladies ("women" being too deceptive a word to tag onto these images) being the next hot favorite.

The images are not the troubling part. It's the messages that folks post about these images that are troubling. America is a country built on the rockiest of race relations. If a fragment of the racial posts is true, the country is in deep shit. It's scary and saddening to see how an entire race or ethnicity can be reduced to a cunt or a cock and an outdated imperialist stereotype. While the technology is dashing into the twenty-first century, the cock is still lurking somewhere in the nineteenth.

PART EIGHT: FINAL

Of course, the Internet is much more than porn and smut. So much more happens on it. But the fear of sex, nudity, and perversion, whatever that is these days, prevails over all else. Ann Landers has been getting oodles of letters about the evils of the Internet and has agreed that 90 percent of the people are only interested in Smut, not politics, arts and culture, or community building and social organizing. Sex is a big scary thing, and if there's one thing the Internet can teach us about sex, if there is one great moral lesson, a universal truth that the Internet can teach us about sex and life, that lesson will be . . .

(STATIC NOISE, SCREEN GOES FUZZY)
(voice-over): Hey, put down the phone, I'm on-line . . . Fuck.
(Fade Out.)

PARDON ME, BUT ARE YOU MR. ASIAN?

Asian America is stuck on the rhetoric of stereotypes. You've heard it all before: Women—passive geisha hooker dragon lady butterfly; Men—sexless nerdy evil Fu Manchu computer technician butterfly. Asian Lesbians—See Women; Asian Gay Men—See Women and Men, add show tunes. Ever since our Asian-American forefathers crawled out of the primeval ooze of the ethnic identity movement, this rhetoric hasn't changed much. Asian America sees itself as exquisite victims, fallen prey to the horrors of these evil stereotypes, and they spend a lot of time and effort to "fight these stereotypes."

Battling the bugbear of stereotypes was one of the goals of the Mr. Asian of Northern California pageant. For the Rice Queens who cannot afford the sex tour to Bangkok this year, this is the second best thing. The boys even have numbers attached to their asses. The only difference is that you can't drag them backstage to suck and fuck for the price of a T-shirt. But, for the price of a calendar, you can take all these shirtless memories home with you, as the contestants have been immortalized in one.

I'm seated behind the Henna Queen and a spit away from four Asian beauty queens. Miss Asian California, Miss Cherry Blossom, Miss Asian Pacific, Miss Asian Universal are decked in their sashes and glittery gowns, but instead of the very essence of glamor, they look like high-priced Thai hookers (except Miss Cherry Blossom, who looks like a Hong Kong lounge hostess), but with tiaras, which is supposed to make all the difference. I am happy to report that none of the beauty queens were showing panty lines through their ultrasheer gowns. I'm most excited to see Miss Asian Universal, because she was recently on *Hard Copy* ratting on Miss Oklahoma Universe, who had been unwittingly exported to Brunei as a blond sex-slave. You know that Miss Asian Universal is a bad chick because she dashed into the show late clutching her Styrofoam container of takeout chow close to her sashed sequined bosom. A beauty queen needs to eat, too.

The wafting strains of Hiroshima's "1,000 Cranes" fade, a hush falls on the auditorium, lights come up on the three cardboard and Styrofoam palm trees on the stage, and the nine contestants, dressed in white T-shirts and green hospital trousers, enter to the prerecorded sounds of Filipino folk music. Every year, the pageant organizers pick an ethnicity to plunder and appropriate, and this year it's the Filipinos. The contestants proceed to do the tinickling, which is a sort of Filipino double-dutch but with two bamboo poles that threaten to smash bare ankles.

The boys look like they have been dragged to Summerfun against their will. There is a lot of laddish jostling, fake grins, and looks of intense concentration as they try not to get their feet caught in the smashing bamboo poles while still trying to smile and remember their introductory lines.

There are nine contestants this year: Allan (use the mike, god-dammit) the Lexus Mechanic, tits, no basket; Luke the Laotian, tits, no basket; Ted the Chiropractor, tits, basket (finally); Alexie with the Crystal Gayle Hair, no tits, no basket; Billy the Biologist with a minor in art, no tits, no basket; Dio Who Might Be Homosexual, tits, basket; Eddie the Hapa, no tits, no basket; Pierre of the Personalitiless I, no tits, no basket; Aaron of the Personalitiless II, no tits, no basket. It's those damn hospital pants that make it hard to show any basket, but haven't these contestants heard of jockstraps and rolled-up socks?

It was damn cruel to make the poor Laotian and the chinkies do all those Filipino dances. Their bodies just weren't made for all that skipping with arms in the air. On one hand, Asian America decries the evil Whiteys lumping Asians all together and thinking that Asians are "all the same," and then there's this.

The emcees for the evening are Pearl and Claire, witless wonders whose main achievements are described in the program booklet. Pearl was a previous beauty queen title holder and model-wanna-be. Claire was in the 1996 Spring Fever Fashion Show (what?). Claire and Pearl introduce the show's organizers, "two powerhouse ladies, Evain and Juana." Doing the twin-cheerleader look, Evain and Juana are wearing the same green dress. After enthusiastic thanks, the two powerhouse ladies whisk off back-stage. "Powerhouse"? Linguistically, Asian-American beauty queens and models are still in the bronze age.

The lights dim and the Soloflex Pull-Up Station is wheeled onto the stage and the poor boys are forced to show their brawn by doing pull-ups, push-ups, and tricep dips. A fifth of their points will be on this effort. Allan the Lexus Mechanic's back pimples are troubling. Ted the Chiropractor is sweating like a hog. Dio Who Might Be Homosexual shakes the whole machine with his efforts. In another less fortunate life, Aaron of the Personalitiless II would be selling noodles in an open-air market. At least the sweat and the exercise is making the lads' nipples harden. You can almost hear the queens (rice, not beauty) drooling. When the last push-up has been pushed, the equipment is wheeled away. Then comes the most anticipated part of all pageants shows: the Talent Portion. The talent falls into three categories: singing, martial arts, and other.

Allan the Lexus Mechanic sings a Temptations song. Could this butch marine with back pimples actually have a high nasal singing voice? He sounds like Prince with a heck of a lot of streptococcus bacteria. The karaoke vibes continue with Pierre of the Personalitiless I, singing a Cantonese song, "I've Got a Date with Spring." Then Dio Who Might Be Homosexual sings "Why God Why" from the smash-hit musical *Miss Saigon*. One day we're being asked to protest against the play, the next day we're singing it at pageants and cultural events. Such mixed messages. Dio Who Might Be Homosexual has the dubious honor of being the only one who uses a scantily clad girl as a stage prop. At the climax of the song he tosses $20 (hey, big spender!) to the sleeping/dead hooker. The audience's reaction is torn between shock at his misogyny and awe at his bodacious machismo.

Since this is an Asian event, martial arts is a very viable talent. Luke the Laotian had promised a poetic recitation ("an ode to his girlfriend") at the press conference but has traded iambic pentamic couplets for nunchaks. Ted the Chiropractor is still sweating like a hog, and it's ruining his dramatic grease-paint makeup. Looking like some bad guy out of *Mortal Kombat* (or *The Power Rangers Turbo* movie), he smashes blocks of plywood to loud cheers from the audience. I'm hoping he will smash blocks of ice with his forehead next. But on trots Aaron of the Personalitiless II, who performs Tiger Crane Kung Fu, and then Billy the Biologist performs Wu-Shu Kung Fu. They both look like bad guys out of Jackie Chan movies, except that Billy demonstrates that he is flexible enough to lick his own balls. Now, that's a talent.

Eddie the Hapa and Alexie with the Crystal Gayle Hair go their own way, the individualists that they are. Alexie with the Crystal Gayle Hair chooses to do a hip-hop techno-dance routine. The music blares from the speakers, the monotonous thumping beat entices a twentieth of the audience to clap along, but they tire out even before the chorus. Alexie with the Crystal Gayle Hair is gyrating to the beat, slapping his crotch, and flinging his Vampira hair with wild Stevie Nicks abandon.

Eddie is more daring. He goes for magic tricks AND dancing. The dancing is stolen from the *Men in Black* video, step for freaking step. The audience cheers when they recognize the shuffling footwork. The magic is a good effort, he makes metal rings interlock (oooooh!), he makes a small rubber ball float in midair (aaaaaaah!), and he makes small flares of red light seemingly appear out of his ass (wow!).

The whole pageant has an aura of a prom gone awry. There is a high-school quality to the whole affair. The audience woofs and catcalls and heckles in sophomoric humor. Evain is clutching a spiral notebook to jot down notes. It is as if the contestants, organizers, and audience are trying desperately to relive their fraternity and sorority days. There is a boyish, immature quality to the evening. Like child beauty pageants, the vibe here is of boys trying to be men to prove some point that few are even sure of.

The show is dragging on, but there is still the other highlight of a pageant: the interview, "where we get to visit the brains behind the brawn," witless Pearl chirps.

The questions are pageant staples: environment, world peace, and love. Witness the brains:

—What are the strongest Asian male characteristics? Allan the Lexus Mechanic: Strong family values, which keep divorce rates down, and Asian males taking care of their elders.
—How do you break down barriers between ethnic groups? Luke the Laotian: By learning a lot from each other and enjoying each other's company.
—What is your opinion of interracial dating? Ted the Chiropractor: Good because you can learn a lot about each other's culture and vice versa.
—What are some of the specific ways to change Asian male stereotypes? Alexie with the Crystal Gayle Hair: A lot of people think Asian males are quiet, but I'm loud! I'm loud and funny, so by being myself, I can change stereotypes!
—Is America a salad bowl or a melting pot? Billy the Biologist: It starts as a salad bowl then becomes a melting pot as we learn more about each other. (It's a freaking tin of fruit cocktail, Billy.)
—What do you appreciate most about your culture? Dio Who Might Be Homosexual: The food and the work ethic.

—What is the most important job in society? Eddie the
  Hapa: Teachers!
—We should strive for world peace, but is war ever justi-
  fiable? Pierre of the Personalitiless I: Only as a last
  resort—when someone threatens our freedom, then we
  should be able to bomb them.
—As the community grows and expands, business also
  needs to grow and expand, but how do we protect the
  environment when business is expanding? Aaron of the
  Personalitiless II: Recycling!

The boys are then made to prance around in their donated tuxe-
dos. They enter the stage to huge slide projections of themselves
posing on a pile of rubble around an abandoned concrete factory.
Aaron of the Personalitiless II seems to be the crowd favorite.

There is more karaoke, with the contestants singing in good-
natured off-key off-tempo karaoke-style, "Hard to Say I'm Sorry"
(it's not that hard, boys, really), and presenting the tearful Evain
and Juana with huge allergy monster bouquets. The results are
tallied. (Drumroll!) The beauty queens are ushered backstage to do
their queenly duties. Mr. Asian of Northern California 1995 shows
us slides of himself sans shirt and yaks about what a great year it
was doing seminude modeling, giving back to the community in
podiatry, expressing pride in Asian heritage, going to the Rose
Bowl Beauty Pageant and having people call him Mr. Asian. He
seems a little drunk, but it could just be the heady thrill of the past
year getting to him.

The huge-ass trophies are hauled out: Allan the Lexus Mechanic wins Mr. Fashion *and* Mr. Congeniality. Alexie with the
Crystal Gayle Hair wins Mr. Photogenic. Ted the Chiropractor

wins Mr. Fitness and First Prince. Billy the Biologist wins Mr. Talent. Eddie the Hapa is Second Prince. And the winner is Dio Who Might Be Homosexual. Hmmm . . . he wasn't fashionable, congenial, fit, talented, or photogenic, but he won. Besides the enviable trophy, he wins $500 and a trip to anywhere in Asia.

Perhaps the organizers and the contestants actually believe that they are combating stereotypes. But what have they actually done? They have shown that Asian men and their cronies in the audience are somehow unable to mature past high-school laddishness. In spite of their efforts, the seminakedness, and the posing, the contestants are not allowed to exude any sense of sexuality, hence their fears of the Asian male being rendered sexless, such an Asian-American conceit, comes true. They have shown that Asians can be as superficial and as mediocre as the bland Pillsbury–Wonder Bread dominant culture of America.

The face of Asian America has changed; there are more Asians who are not so crippled by the notion of stereotypes or of someone else's perceptions. Stereotypes are about how someone else sees you, but Asian America seems to have taken the shame and blame for someone else's perceptions and tried to live against it. There is nothing wrong with being passive, geisha, hooker, dragon lady, butterfly, sexless, nerdy, evil, Fu Manchu, or computer technician *if that is really what one is*; but there is something wrong in trying to overcompensate so that someone else's ignorance is not validated. There is more at stake for Asian America than beauty.

During the pageant, witless Claire says, "Wow, these contestants have a lot going for them!" and at that point, a stagehand who was moving props let out an audible guffaw. I'm sure these contestants are fine human beings (or at least one hopes that they are or will be), but in the middle of this wreck of failed intentions, it's difficult not to agree with that definitive "Ha!" in the dark.

POSTSCRIPT

I thought that I had written a tongue-in-cheek, decidedly ironic piece on the Mr. Asian of Northern California pageant, and I was unprepared for the wrath that would befall me after the piece was published on the *Bay Guardian*'s on-line web site. Apparently, many of the organizers and contestants did not see any irony, humor, or tongues in the piece.

While many of the organizers and board members fired off irate letters to the editors, the bulk of chastising me was laid at the newly crowned Mr. Asian's feet. In his first act as Mr. Asian 1997, he fired off a three-page letter to the editors which they reprinted on-line.

It was titled "Pardon Me, That's Mr. Asian to You, If You're Nasty." I wasn't particularly sure what the dated Janet Jackson reference was supposed to mean, except that Mr. Asian 1997 is a fan of Ms. Jackson. Mr. Asian 1997 was dead pissed, and he aimed all barrels at me and my entire writing and performance life of the last five years.

"When I recently read Mr. Chin's three page (sic) article on his take on the Mr. Asian competition I began to feel like (here we go again) I've been deported back into a time warp, into a world where boys do 'lick their own balls,' temptresses incite you to 'Lick My Butt' (a title of one of his poems), prostitutes reign hugging their toilet thrones, and for a Finale everybody gets dragged backstage 'to fuck

for a price of a T-shirt.' In his world, brothers kill brothers and mothers eat their youngs (sic). There are no redeeming qualities in the characters or in the writing. Forever stuck in some Asian American version of Boys in the Band . . . When I read this joke of a journalistic piece of verbal diarrhea, I begin to feel like he is collecting material for his next piece of sensationalist contribution to the same collection of short stories and magazines. You must be desperate for new material, Chin, to come to our press release in your fisherman hat (must be a markdown sale at Buffalo Exchange)."

Short note of explanation: I had dyed my hair a regretful punkish red and did not want to show up at the press conference looking like some scrappy little biker-chick. So I nipped into the Gap and bought a hat that was on sale to stuff my head under. Mr. Asian 1997's ire gets more pointed.

"You may be blinded by your anger but you have become what you loathed so much in your stereotypes: Bitter and angry, but still a Madame Butterfly (potato queen); Aria fades."

"Mr. Chin warns us not 'to overcompensate for the ignorance of others' yet he has profited from these same words. Like the newly appointed overseer 'Uncle Tom' in the plantation, he has learned to wave the master's whip by so readily mixing the same deadly concoction."

"I've heard you laugh before at your own self deprecating (sic) humor that nobody relates or appreciates anymore. Warning: We are approaching the millennium and you are not getting any younger. And you are no beauty queen."

I am completely aware that I am not any beauty queen by any standard, but that was one of the points I was trying to make. That somehow, in the queer community and in the Asian community, a porno star is held in higher esteem than a writer, that bitchiness and name-calling is taken for wit, and looks will get you anything and anywhere. The one thing in Mr. Asian 1997's tirade that I do take offense at had little to do with me.

"(By the way, the controversy behind Miss Saigon was the fact that a white man played an Asian role. Obviously, you missed the subtle difference in this case. Next time read the entire article and not just the Headlines!)"

Actually, the protests against *Miss Saigon* were about the casting *and* the depiction of Asian women and the notion that their killing and sacrificing themselves for their white lovers was a conventional romantic plot line. Not such a subtle difference. Mr. Asian 1997's limited reading and his condemnation of how I interpreted the *Miss Saigon* brouhaha underscores how we see issues in different ways. Just as the ire directed toward my review for the *Bay Guardian* showed. Some people saw the show as a powerful statement of identity politics; I saw a simple, regular beauty pageant and a completely ludicrous display of Asian machismo that problematized identity politics if anyone even cared about the event. The event was less than a sellout. And when I had asked one of the organizers what Mr. Asian did in his tenure, she told me that he did not do much; most parades and street festivals or cultural festivals prefer to have any one of the dozens of Miss Asians to grace their fete.

Mr. Asian 1997's use of *Miss Saigon* in his talent portion, and the way he staged his song, was interesting. I had known of Mr. Asian 1997 before and knew that he was gay. He had volunteered his time and energies in the gay Asian community, and I was surprised to see him passing as straight. In all fairness, he was *acting*. The pageant was decidedly a heterosexual event. The nudge-nudge quality of sexual innuendo, beauty queens, and emcee's remarks all smacked of an unquestioned heterosexual abandon. So I thought it was interesting to witness a person I knew was gay participating in such an event with his sexuality hidden or at least obscured. Even in his rabid response, he never offered that he was gay. I did not care to out him, so I offhandedly referred to him as "Who Might Be Homosexual," which offended him as much as anything else. I thought it was interesting that someone who had placed such a stake in identity politics would pass as nongay. Would it have mattered to the pageant if they knew he was gay? Or did he feel that the knowledge that he was gay would somehow threaten his masculinity, his maleness, his mister-ness, in the judges' eyes? Would the judges have felt that way?

In spite of his name-calling and ad hominem attacks, Mr. Asian 1997 did raise some interesting and arguable points in his note. He writes:

> *"And I think that there is something wrong with your assertion that we should accept being passive, geisha, a dragon lady because nobody chooses to be that unless someone's (sic) else's perception shames you to live that life."*

Being passive, sexual, asexual, nerdy, driven, domineering, or even inscrutable (look it up) is not a bad thing, if that is really one's personality. There is no shame in that. I find it interesting and troubling that there are Asian-Americans who believe that they are such exquisite victims of the evil domineering society that they will, in a fey swoon, without any resistance, fall into "that life."

How the pageant played itself out was very much what my point was about. The participants have on their minds the stereotype that Asians are feminine, effeminate, or emasculated, and so, the pageant goes out of its way to emphasize the contestants' maleness. What does masculinity mean in this context then? What does an Asian-American masculinity mean? And is it really that important, and to whom? The "community"? The contestants? Are Asian-American men so insecure that they need this pageantry of staged machismo to pat themselves on the back or head and to comfort themselves that they might just be normal? Mr. Asian 1997 continues:

> *"The face of Asian America has changed. Despite your jadedness, I believe that the rhetoric must continue because each generation must enter the doors of discussion and define its place in this ever-changing landscape.*
>
> *"And it is vital that we remember our past mistakes so that future generations will sway from the worst of our faces which you have so shamelessly shown us."*

The rhetoric continues like an endless loop, a CD player stuck on the replay button. Much of Asian America is still harping on the same platitudes from the last few decades: the evil White Man, evil sexually predatory Rice Queens, Whitey's perceptions of Asians, and bad media stereotypes. The rhetoric is not as simple as white and yellow, good and bad; and Asian-Americans are not the blameless victims they have been taught to believe.

While I appreciate the history and the struggle of Asian-Americans, there are many people that now live in America who do not have similar frames of reference of growing up in America. Many of these people, including myself, feel excluded and untouched by the art and culture created out of those references. I am a transplanted person who remembers something of where I came from, where I am now, and where I can go—personally, politically, and artistically.

As the dynamics and demographics of the United States change, we find that more and more hybrid states of being and desire are created. It is the future of this country, of ourselves. How we look at ourselves and, hence, how we look at others will be vastly changed. Each generation need not go through the same discussion; the discourse must move forward.

Mr. Asian 1997 ends his missive, just as all the other irate letters to the editor did. He challenged me to join the pageant the next year. It is like saying that you should not tell someone to stick themselves in the eye with a sharp stick until you've actually done it yourself. Besides, I'm no beauty queen. That talent is best left to those who feel that they are.

SMILE

Known as The Land of Smiles, Thailand has long had the aura of a free-and-easy sex market. Ever since the late sixties, when soldiers fighting in the war in Vietnam came en masse to Thailand for their R&R, the mystique and reputation of Thailand for such sexual pleasures have grown. The advent of AIDS has cast a pall on the sexual shenanigans of the place, but is still a mere drizzle on the parade. A reputation is hard to live down. Every year, Thailand is visited by more than five million tourists. According to the Thai government, 67 percent of these tourists are single men, and in a recent survey, one-third said they intended to have sex with a Thai while on their trip. In a German *Playboy* magazine, a survey found that 56 percent of those polled dream of sexual relations with Asian women and 22 percent have taken sex tours to Thailand. By the Thai government's estimates, there are at least 100,000 prostitutes working in the country; social workers believe there are many more. A large percentage of these are young men and women, some barely out of their teens, or even younger. Currently, the

Thai government reports that there are 200,000 to 400,000 Thais who are HIV-infected. AIDS workers believe the number is close to 500,000, 1 percent of the population. By the year 2000, the World Health Organization says that there will be two million to four million Thais, 6 percent of the population, infected by the AIDS virus, and one out of every three deaths will be AIDS-related. The spread of AIDS has risen sharply in Thailand. In 1985, there were only five *registered* cases; by 1990, there were 25,000 cases. A year later, the number had risen to 33,000.

In Bangkok's famed Patpong district, the gay establishments and the straight ones seem to coexist in harmony. By evening, the street vendors and food sellers have stalked their spots on the strip and the place is packed with stalls selling anything from knock-off designer watches and clothes to tourist trinkets and jewelry. Beggars, old crippled men and women, some cradling little children, sit in the nooks between stalls and beg for money. Amputees push themselves along on makeshift rollers begging, too. In the muggy throng, touts are everywhere trying to lure potential customers. Some work for an establishment by standing directly outside the door of the club carrying little photo albums or composite sheets of the young men and women who work inside. The doors are usually cracked open so that you can get a titillating glimpse inside. Other touts are freelancers, working for a number of establishments, and they will escort you to a bar or club that caters to your area of interest. The touts all carry little tattered laminated fold-out sheets no larger than a bus schedule that lists the prices and the act: anything from a floor show to a massage to a hand job.

The clubs and bars are named after American blockbusters: the

Mask, Superman, Seven, Midnight Cowboy; or suggestively: Golden Cock. For the heterosexuals, it's Suzie Wong, Superpussy, and Hot Stuff. Subtlety is not the key here.

If you think the sex trade in Thailand is aimed at the European or Western tourists, it's only because these tourists stand out in the crowds. The Asian tourists blend in, but their presence and dollars are still sought after. This is evidenced by the touts carrying signs in Chinese, Korean, and Japanese. Especially Japanese.

If you're still lost for choices, your *tuk-tuk* man, the operator of the little motorized pedicabs, can help you. He will often insist on taking you on a detour from your destination. Since pictures speak louder than words and certainly need less translation or present less room for error, he will show you a pictorial selection of where he might take you: It's like ordering by number from a McDonald's menu.

Over at the Mask, where the sign has been copied right down to the typeface of the movie posters, the shows are just starting. The boys are wearing club-issued T-shirts with a drawing of a masked Jim Carrey on the back.

The young man at the door tells me what's on for the night. First, there's the Masturbating Show, where the boys line up on stage and masturbate without actually ejaculating. Then comes the Candlestick Show, where a boy dances with fistfuls of house candles, dripping wax over his body. Next, it's the Shower Show: two boys on a sudsy stage complete with a rain curtain. This is followed by the main attraction, the Fucking Show. A boy dressed as a girl is fucked on stage by a masked boy. At the onset of the show, the masked boy makes a show of clumsily putting on two condoms before he does his act.

Then the boys are back onstage. The waiters work as middlemen, persuading and cajoling you to go with a boy. If you want to go with a boy, you simply point him out to a waiter or request him by the number pinned to his T-shirt or underwear, and the waiter will send for him. Drinks will have to be bought, of which the boy gets a small cut. Then the negotiations begin. First, there is an off-bar fee, or a "takeout" fee, to allow the boy to stop working, this will be about 200 baht. (US $1 is equal to about 25 Thai baht.) This fee will allow you to leave with the boy or go to a backroom with him. Now you negotiate for either a short term or a long term. A short term will cost anywhere from 500 to 700 baht and the boy will need to be back at work in a couple of hours; a long term—an overnighter, will cost about 1,800 baht. If you like, the club can rent you a room at the back of the bar for an additional 200 baht. Then there are tips. It all adds up.

The room is a dingy affair. A tattered mattress, your choice of a red light bulb or fluorescent lighting, framed pictures of some-one's birthday party, and a roll of toilet paper to clean up with. The boy is given some condoms that are wrapped in newspaper. The boys are between 18 and 25 here, I'm told. In all the bars, no one will fess up to being younger than 18 or older than 25.

Goh is twenty-four years old and he has been working at the Mask for two months. He came to Bangkok when he was 19 to look for work. He started out as a cook, but, like so many others, found that being a go-go boy was more lucrative. He works as much as every day of the month and gets every fifth day off if he chooses. For this, he is paid 1,200 baht a month; tips will make up the rest. He doesn't speak much English and is embarrassed by it. "No style," he laughs apologetically. All his transactions and ne-gotiations will have to take place through an intermediary: his bosses at the bar and his chums who work there. His bosses say that he'll "do anything, whatever you want, you just tell me." Goh doesn't really like to be fucked in the ass, but his bosses say he can be persuaded for the right amount of money. For a tip, his friends at the club are also willing to help mediate his transactions.

Down the street, at the Superman A-Go-Go, it's more homely. The mama-san will tell you which boys will do what sex acts, who will allow themselves to have anal sex and who won't. There are no shows here, just a raised platform in the middle of the room where a rotation of three boys will be standing naked and bobbing to late eighties disco music. They are buck naked and stand with their underwear clutched in a wad in one hand while the other hand is either uninterestedly tugging at their penis or simply covering their crotch. Here, the fees are much cheaper, as there aren't shows to put on. It's a flat 500 baht plus whatever you want to tip the boy, 200 baht more if you want the room. In comparison, a draft beer will cost you 180 baht.

The mama-san tells me that here boys are all clean and that they go for health checkups and blood tests every week. Most of the guys are in school or in university and do this to earn additional money. "What ages do you want? I got 18, 19, 20, 25," she says. When the boys are off the stage, they sit in a small alcove behind the main club area. Here in the dugout, they prime their penises while watching straight porn on a small television.

On the other end of the spectrum, there is the Jupiter, a classy establishment complete with a Greco-Roman motif. The Jupiter is known for its floor shows: fire-dancing and eating, a fluorescent body-paint dance, oiled men who grope and caress each other, and a priapic parade of the boys whose penises are tied off at the base to maintain their huge erections. Then, holding on to their engorged penises, they walk single file through the bar crowds.

The Fucking Show here is also more elaborate, more showy. The anal-insertive boy will carry his partner, impaled on his penis, out into the audience, lay the boy on the laps of the bar patrons, and continue to fuck him until a small gratuity is paid. The show ends with a big flourish: the boy, still being carried around, blowing kisses to the audience as they exit to count their cash.

At the Jupiter, there is only a takeout fee, no rooms to rent. The boy works as a free agent. He is not paid a salary. The club makes its off-bar fee of 200 baht if someone wants to leave with a boy. You have to then negotiate with the boy himself. The usual range being 1,000 baht for a short term and this does not include a hotel room and additions like cab fares, drinks, dinner for him (and possibly a chum).

Ken is a twenty-five-year-old university student. He has been in Bangkok for three months, and on recommendations of his friends, he got to work at the Jupiter. Hired because he's beefy and muscular rather than well endowed, he's not in the shows, but is only a go-go boy. The performers *do* get a small salary for their showmanship, but the go-go boys really need to hustle. Still, it's a good job, he says, it's flexible, and he makes a good amount of money. He's not too concerned about his safety going with complete strangers to their rooms, nor about contracting sexually transmitted diseases. He feels he can take care of the situation by his wits and brawn. He says he can see if someone is diseased or not. And even then, it sure beats the hell out of waiting tables, working construction, or a stuffy office job at a tenth of the pay.

If a boy chooses this career path, he has to make his money while he still has his youth, anything over 25 is washed up in the business. If you can't work in the bars, then it's off to the parks, bathhouses, and street hustling, where, hopefully, he'll meet someone who will provide some financial security.

For the more motivated and brassy who do not like the confines of the club scene, there are bars. At Harry's Bar, there are no go-go boys. Instead, there are bar boys. Chai is twenty-four years old. By day, he works at a company importing DKNY clothes. By night, he works as a bar boy. He calls it his "hobby" and supplements his income by "making friends and making money from my friends." Harry's also offers dismal rooms above the bar at 200 baht a pop. The bar itself is decorated with framed pictures clipped out from American porn magazines. Chai doesn't actually get paid for hanging out in the bar, what he makes from his "friends" is what he makes. To achieve this, he'll flatter you and grope you. Don't think it's because of your beguiling charms or even your less tangible qualities. Everyone is treated like this. Even the most odious lump of flesh that sashays through the door will be greeted and fawned over with groping, whispered flattery, and suggestive little kisses on the neck and propositions to go upstairs.

While it is easy to tut-tut at the foreigners with fat wallets, the balance of this trade is more delicate than good and bad, native and colonial, or East and West. For every foreigner who screws around, there are well-meaning ones, too. And whole families are being supported by the graces of a boy's relationship with a richer expatriate or tourist. In the mid-eighties, a lot of the information about AIDS and safer sex was culled from foreigners and tourists. Today, as safer sex education in Thailand remains either unclear or inaccessible (illiteracy rates are high in the provinces), this exchange of information becomes more vital. Then again, for a long time, backed with a fierce denial, Thailand refused to acknowledge the presence of AIDS, decrying it as a foreign disease, and, often, customers felt that if they paid a good amount of money or if they had sex with "virgins" and younger boys, they would be immune and the sex industry was only too happy to cater to that delusion. Superstition also abounded: Drinking cobra's blood or certain medicinal herbs were thought to protect one from contracting the AIDS virus. Even in neighboring Singapore, where the populace is arguably more educated and more economically sound, a recent newspaper survey at an AIDS awareness exhibition found that 50 percent of the people surveyed did not know the basics of safer sex and how HIV is transmitted.

Today, in Bangkok, the idea of safer sex is certainly in the air, as the governmental and nongovernmental organizations have done a great deal to spread the word on AIDS education. Organizations like the Fraternity for AIDS Cessation in Thailand (FACT, which has been around since 1986) have done a lot of outreach in bars, in and outside of Bangkok, and in the Thai military and schools to educate sex workers and their potential customers about using condoms to prevent sexually transmitted diseases. They provide the clubs with free packs of condoms. In any fucking show, the boys will use two condoms. In 1992 the government handed out 70 million condoms, and their surveys showed that condom use among customers was up by 60 percent compared to five years ago. Still, when the bedroom or backroom door is shut, no one really knows if safer sex is being practiced.

And even as the incidence of AIDS among heterosexuals rises, and the numbers in gay circles decrease, this means little as sexual identity is not as highly demarcated as it is in the West. Often you will find horny married men at gay saunas looking for quick sex, or a gay man who is married to a woman living in a gay relation with a man. Often, the boys working in the clubs and go-go bars do not define themselves as gay, and many have girlfriends or are married.

But with a $5 billion tourist industry at stake—with ties to airlines, tour operators, hotels, and smaller businesses—the government doesn't want to rock the boat too much. There is an expectation that some kind of sexual trade will happen. Hotels, even ritzy ones like the Holiday Inn and Marriott, specify a charge of half a night's rate for bringing a guest up to the room in the evening. It's arguable whether this is to make money off the sex trade or to discourage it.

While sex tourism gave AIDS its initial wave of infections in the country, it is no longer a major factor in the spread of the disease, proclaims Viravaidya Meechai, a government minister who used to head the Thai safer sex efforts, at a World Bank's AIDS seminar. "AIDS is being spread by Thais within Thailand. The moral argument is stronger than the epidemiological argument. We cannot find evidence that tourism is a major route of infection either into a country or out of it."

According to the World Health Organization, AIDS in Asia is usually spread by Asian-to-Asian contact, and more than 75 percent of all infections are from heterosexual sex and a large percentage are also from intravenous drug use. And it continues to spread throughout Asia at alarming rates. It is estimated that more than 10 million Asians will be infected by the end of the century.

What is to be done remains to be argued. Given the precarious nature of Thai politics, governments and administrations come in and out of power and favor every so often, and this strains the continuity of any program to tackle the steadfast sex trade or the spread of AIDS. Many governments, like those in Australia and Germany, have passed some kind of legislation to prevent the sexual exploitation of children in other countries, where a person caught sexually exploiting minors abroad can be tried according to the laws of his native country.

Several years ago, a Thai government official said that the sex trade would taper off as the country got more economically stable, but even after the booming eighties, the country is still sharply divided between rich and poor. In the city, little shacks and squatter huts line palatial houses and country clubs, and young men and women work in shopping malls selling consumer items they can't afford to buy.

Pattaya is a two-hour drive from Bangkok. Located on the east coast on the Gulf of Thailand, Pattaya used to be the sex capital of Southeast Asia. Since then, its reputation has slipped; it has gained somewhat of a seedy reputation, and having at one time boasted the highest HIV rate in the world hasn't helped. Tourists now prefer to go to Chiang Mai or Phuket; Southeast Asian tourists flock to Hat Yai. Since then, the Pattaya government has cracked down on the sex industry. They want the city to be seen as a family holiday spot again. But still, the place is driven by sex and sexual desire. There are more bars per square foot than anywhere else. The town survives on tourism and shore leave. Everywhere, banners proclaim that establishments "Welcome the U.S. Navy." There are bars that cater specifically to Aussie, Brit, German, and Russian navies.

The boom days of Pattaya are legendary. There is the area of

Jomtien beach, well-known for its pedophile activity where, for the right price, pedophiles may have their way with boys as young as seven or eight years old. Most pedophiles have moved on to newer pastures like Sri Lanka, Cambodia, and Ho Chi Minh City. While the government has curbed any overt pedophile activities, the number of young boys who run around the outdoor patios of gay bars to sell little trinkets and to play with the tourists certainly arouses some unsettling suspicions.

Right now, it is the low tourist season, and many of the boys have gone home to their respective towns to other jobs and will return in a few months, at the end of the year, when the tourist season picks up. Those who remain probably have regular customers whom they are expecting.

Most of the gay bars are congregated in a small L-shaped lane nicknamed Boystown. There is a wooden signboard stretching from one side of the street to the other that lists the bars there: the Cockpit, Cocobanana, Pub Amor, and Boys Boys Boys. Down the street it's the Bodyguard, the A-Bomb, Stars, and Many Boys.

Since it's the low tourist season, each bar employs about 40 to 50 boys, but with only 4 or 5 tourists in an establishment at any given time, the go-go boys far outnumber the tourists at this time of the year. Being in a club feels like being in Hitchcock's *The Birds*. During the peak season, one bar manager tells me, a club may hire up to as many as 100 to 120 boys and most of them will be taken each night.

Hiring for a club is not easy, the manager tells me. He needs to take into consideration the balance of every kind of boy—how many femmy ones, how many muscle boys; what sexual act they are willing to do—in a twist of Western gayspeak, gay kings and gay queens; and the bar's primary patrons—how many dark-skinned and light-skinned, since "the Europeans like the dark ones and the Japanese like the light ones."

I ask him how the boys come to work here. Is there an audition, does the club actively seek these young men out? "No need." He laughs. The boys are usually friends of someone who already works there and who recommends him, or they simply know the score and come in and ask to work there.

I mention how I read that some straight bars buy young girls as indentured workers, or how some parents sell their youngest daughters to bars, and I wondered if this ever happened in the gay sex trade. He is genuinely offended and categorically denies that such things ever happen in the gay bars. The boys can come and go as they please, he says. Well, maybe in some other less major tourist areas, maybe that happens, but not in Pattaya, and, he insists, not in any club he knows.

Ask any of the boys working in the go-go bars why they do this and they will tell you it's because they can make gobs more money than a regular office or service-industry job. A large number are not very well-educated, and this is one of the better job opportunities for them. Some, like Ken at the Jupiter in Bangkok, are working their way through university. It is not an even-paying field: Someone like Ken is in a better position to negotiate and bargain for his money and work conditions, unlike Goh at the Mask, who is clearly being ripped off by his buddies and his bosses. How they feel about their job is a tougher question and a harder one for them to answer: It's a job, nothing more than that. Some will say they hope to meet a nice man who will take care of them. Most of the boys in Pattaya, or Bangkok for that matter, are not gay in the Western sense of the word. Getting into their undies or less onstage and entertaining tourists is all part of a job. It's interesting to see their girlfriends coming to pick them up after work or, in some cases, hanging out in the clubs, holding on to their boyfriend's cigarettes and bag.

Surprisingly, gay men are not the only ones who patronize these bars. In Pattaya, there are a number of European and Japanese women buying the services of these boys, too. The takeout fee is a standard 200 baht. Not much sense in price-cutting or overcharging here. All else is negotiated. In Pattaya, the game is a little different; the town is much smaller than Bangkok, and the bars and clubs seem to have a more standard approach to their flesh trade. When a boy sits with a customer and gets the customer to buy him a drink, which will cost 80 to 100 baht, the boy will get a small cut, usually 10 baht. When he shows up for work, he is paid a token 100 baht. If he leaves with a customer, he might be paid 50 baht of the "takeout fee," and whatever he can convince the customer he is worth. If no one takes him for the night, he returns that 100 baht. The bars in Pattaya don't usually have rooms, but don't worry if you're hard-pressed for a place to take your new friend. Many of the coffee shops and restaurants have little rooms for rent.

In the old days, a customer tells me, go-go bars used to have cubicles behind the general seating area so that customers could check out the goods before leaving with a boy. But all that is gone now, he says, sighing.

If you want to be discreet, you can go across town to the northern end of Pattaya to Adam & Eve. Decorated with big paintings of gay Hollywood icons on the walls, Adam & Eve is a classy joint. It's also well-known for its lavish drag cabaret shows. They even have two boys working the rest rooms who will put a hot towel on your neck and give you a back massage while you are pissing at the urinal. You have to tip them for this service, of course. Adam & Eve is so classy, the boys don't even have to strip down to their club-issued underwear to flaunt their goods. They get to stay in their street clothes, smoking cigarettes onstage waiting to be picked. The club offers massages: 300 baht for a hand massage, or 500 baht for something called a "body to body soap massage." "It's like nothing you have ever felt before," a fortyish Singaporean customer tells me. Apparently, the boy will squish liquid soap over your body and he will use his body to slither and slide over you. The boys will even pay the owner a small fee to teach them this particular skill before working there.

Adam & Eve prides itself on its level of discretion. A customer can leave his table and go upstairs with a boy without anyone actually seeing anything out of the ordinary. There are many exits and backstairs all laid out in bad sixties spy-movie fashion to assure such discretion.

At Stars, Thap tells me that he had a boyfriend from America before, a teacher from Texas. He complains about the slow season and how much he would prefer to work at Adam & Eve but he is not buffed enough. How does he make his living in the low tourist season? I ask. He tells me that he has savings, some friends who help him out, and a part-time job as a waiter. Besides, it's not as expensive as living in Bangkok, he says. He's unafraid of AIDS. He knows about safer sex, he says. He will practice it until he's certain the person "is okay."

Bars and clubs will hire certain types of looks. And if you don't suit the look you have to find other ways to make your money. Another sexual commerce involves young girls who putt around on mopeds along Pattaya's strip looking for single men to offer their friendship and a "Thai massage" to. It's a gig that mostly young girls do. A few transsexuals get in on the gig, too.

Mallee is a twenty-four-year-old transsexual. She looks like any one of the bargirls, with her heavily powdered face, super-red lipstick, and tight black minidress. In the harsh daylight, she looks a frightful sight. The only thing that tips one off is the slight Adam's apple, and some broad, manly features in her face. She works at a massage parlor in a Bangkok hotel but likes to make these little excursions to Pattaya to make a bit of extra cash. In Pattaya, she rents a small windowless room at 50 baht a day behind a shophouse to ply her trade. Massage parlors are usually covers for brothels, but the hotel in Bangkok is on the up-and-up, she insists. She came to Bangkok to make a living, and had the usual run-of-the-mill jobs: waitress, shop assistant—but working in a massage parlor seemed to be the best way to make good money. The parlor trained her for free, too. She has a small family up north to whom she sends some money. They know what she does for a living. Why shouldn't they? There's nothing wrong with giving massages, she says, slightly offended. The Thai massage culminates in a hand job, so there's little chance of her hidden gender being found out if she doesn't go any further. She ultimately dreams of meeting a good American bloke and coming to America to live in luxury, she says. But in the meantime, she just wants to make enough money to live comfortably.

With all the competition around from other boys and bars, it's constant hustle. From the moment you approach the bar, there is always someone assigned to cajole you and persuade you to go with a boy. The best tactic is a hurt and surprised hangdog expression when you say you don't want to go with one of their boys. The boys who are on the good side of the waiters and captains tend to do better, as they will be recommended to a customer.

When a boy does get a customer, he will try to go in for the kill. The best kinds of customers I'm told are those that are staying for a week or more. Hopefully, the customer will want the boy's company for the duration of his stay. What this means is that the customer will take care of the boy's meals, shopping (name-brand jeans, jewelry, and leather goods are much sought after), and any other little presents to show his affection. There is talk of how one lucky boy managed to get a motorbike, which he promptly resold after the man left. It is not uncommon for the boys to keep in touch with their friend from abroad, to whom they will write asking for money because a mother or a grandmother is ill and needs medication or is dying. Some grandmothers have been dying repeatedly for the last three years.

In a 1992 survey, the Thai government estimated that there are more than 76,800 sex workers (men and women) working at 5,600 establishments. Of these, 20,300 sex workers are working at 680-odd establishments in Bangkok. Activists pooh-pooh these numbers as being highly conservative.

It is hard to put a finger down on the numbers or on the scene itself, as it is an ever-changing beast. Bars and businesses come and go. Just a year ago, the guidebook listed something called a Night Hunter tour that promised "cruising in a specially equipped van with tinted windows, bed and guide. Visit park, sauna, and cinema. 7-hour tour." Now that's gone and the irate woman at the other end of the line doesn't know where to go.

Advocates of Thailand will tell you that the sexual culture and the flesh trade are only small aspects of the culture—a small drop in the bucket of the whole country. They'll tell you that Thailand is more than available boys and girls that may be bought for the price of a six-pack, that sex for money is certainly not unique to Thailand, and that the write-ups about Thailand's sex trade in the Western press are horridly sensationalistic and unfair.

"The sex tourism is a sensationalization of the international media. The number of people who go to Thailand for the sex trade is small. The vast majority of tourists who go to Thailand are interested in sight-seeing, shopping and relaxing," insists Eric Allyn, author of *The Men of Thailand Guide to Thailand.*

"The commercial sex gay scene is a tiny, albeit fascinating, part of Thailand. Most foreigners get it out of their system in the first night or two and are ready to do the tourist scene. Thailand is certainly more easygoing about people's private sex lives, but it is not a big sex club."

While Allyn may possibly be right, a reputation—culled from decades of hearsay, mass media, and advertising—is hard to live down. And the Thai tourist industry's media campaigns and advertisements certainly use that reputation, wrapped in sexual innuendo and titillation to sell their country as a vacation hot spot.

The gay sex trade in Thailand is a mix of mythology, fantasy, and stereotypes. Many of the boys look very young, barely out of their teens. They'll tell you that they are twenty-three or twenty-four years old. It's hard to believe but no one is about to ask for

IDs. The conventional wisdom is that Asians generally tend to "look young." Customers and businesses are more than willing to buy into this stereotype and party on with a knowing wink.

In all this talk about sex, sex in the real sense of that word seems to be missing from the picture. The boys who work at these bars are really young men. But they still look like boys and exhibit a boyish demeanor which makes their "sex acts" a little disconcerting. They simply come across as boys horsing around or playing doctor. They giggle and laugh at each other when one is onstage, or cheer each other on when a friend is doing an act. There is good-natured jostling and elbowing. At one club, one of the boys sneaks behind a pillar and gooses his friend. When they are onstage, they display as much enthusiasm as they would studying calculus on a hot summer afternoon. They go through the motions, but somehow, some of their penises still remain disinterested and flaccid no matter how much they tug at them.

At the Jupiter, a young man is on stage in a solo masturbation show. He is sitting in a deck chair with fake Ray-Ban sunglasses on and has been masturbating for a good ten minutes. At one point, there is loud guffawing from the dugout, and the boy looks over forlornly like he wishes he were sharing in their play, instead of trying to ejaculate to a difficult and unappreciative crowd. He finally stands up, ejaculates, takes a bow to polite applause, and leaves.

These sex acts are meant to arouse and impel one's loins to some sexual desire, but it all ends up having the manner of a high-school play production.

The issue of gay sex tourism in Thailand, and around the world, is at best overlooked in the gay community.

To begin with, sex tourism is very much a heterosexual activity. Most of the documentation, media reports, and discourse have focused on the heterosexual sex trade. Pedophilic organizations and activities, in the United States and abroad, are also very much heterosexual. Reports of gay sex tourism do not make the reading racks as often as accounts of heterosexual shenanigans. Still, gay sex tourism has existed for a long time: Think back to gay literature twenty-five years ago when authors wrote of going to Morocco or Italy to enjoy some exotic, young, dark-skinned boy.

Many politically aware people, activists, and academics know the issue only marginally and haven't thought about it much; hence, declining to offer any comment for this article. For those who broach the issue, they find themselves on thorny ground. Many different issues collude in this one issue, not the least of which are consent, individual autonomy, and labor conditions. On a more theoretical level, the issues of privilege, power relations, and economic dominance are certainly not easy ones to tackle.

Julie Dorf, director of the International Lesbian and Gay Human Rights Commission, explains: "There is a fear of being antisex in any way. It's a really complicated issue and having an antisex approach isn't going to help. It's difficult in a movement that is being attacked from so many different directions because of the actual sex acts that we perform and engage in, and there's so much homophobia that we deal with that it's very hard to have a position that would, in some way, seem not sexually revolutionary or liberatory."

Discussing sex tourism is made difficult because of the element of child prostitution. End Child Prostitution in Asian Tourism (ECPAT), a Christian-based coalition of children's advocates, estimates that there are 200,000 child prostitutes, boys and girls, in

Thailand, 400,000 in India, and 60,000 in the Philippines. But as Thailand and the Philippines crack down on child prostitution in the face of global criticism, and with the frightening reports of the prevalence of AIDS there, many pedophiles are moving off to other newly developing countries, like Sir Lanka, Goa, Vietnam, Cambodia, and Burma. Often too, young men and women are transported across borders to other countries to work the sex trade. The Cambodian Women's Development Organization reports that there has been a large increase in homosexual child prostitution.

While some activists will fiercely condemn sex with children, they may not have the same problem with young adults working in the sex industry. The sticky part is when it comes to sex with teenagers. This is because age-of-consent laws, and what consent actually is, are brought into question.

This is where the case of Dr. Gavin Scott comes in. Scott, a British physician who has lived and practiced medicine in Cambodia since 1992, was arrested and charged with the attempted rape of five teenage boys last year. He was convicted in a Phnom Penh court and received a suspended sentence of two years, of which he served five months, and ordered to pay restitution to the boys.

In court, the boys' ages were stated to be under fifteen. Scott said they told him they were over sixteen and that he paid them to have sex. "They were lying. Everyone knows the bloody boys are prostitutes," Scott said during his trial.

Later, in a letter published by the *Cambodia Daily*, Scott charged that the whole affair was "a case against homosexuality, but was misrepresented as a case about child sex."

"I deplore pedophilia. I'm the victim. The real issue is not pedophilia but homosexuality," he wrote. Scott's arrest was made when authorities were tipped off by a nongovernmental agency, and he feels that the agencies involved, which include ECPAT and a local Cambodian human-rights group, placed undue pressure on the press and tribunal. "Ask how many of their targets are homosexual. Ask why they are persecuting a man whose alleged guilt revolves around a few months separating a 15 year old (sic) and a 16-year-old when they could more easily prosecute real pedophiles."

The agencies tersely replied that Scott's charges of homophobia were unfounded and that it was simply a matter of the children being under the age of consent.

While Dr. Scott was prosecuted, perhaps to make an example of him, many others are not. Even when caught, they bribe their way out of it, or simply leave the country. In response to this, many countries have laws that will allow a country to prosecute a citizen who has sex with an underage person abroad. Germany, Australia, Belgium, and Sweden have all actively prosecuted men who have had sex with minors in Asia. In the US, the Child Sex Abuse Prevention Act which was passed more than a year ago makes it a felony for a US citizen or permanent resident traveling abroad to engage in sexual acts with a minor. Twenty-two of the ninety-six pedophiles tried and convicted in the Philippines, Thailand, and Sri Lanka between 1986 and 1992 were US citizens. "It's outrageous that US citizens can travel abroad and exploit and abuse minors in a way that is illegal in the US," said Joseph Kennedy (D-Mass.), one of the cosponsors of the bill.

Many agencies and nongovernmental organizations exist to defend the rights of children, but these children and street kids soon grow up, and while they may be legally of the age of consent, they are still barely into their teens. The conditions for a boy working in an expensive go-go club are quite different from a boy being pimped in a park or locked in a brothel.

Sex workers are clearly having their human rights violated when they are sold into the sex trade or are coerced into it in any way, Dorf said. So are the workers who lack the control over their working conditions, including the number of clients, and who are being denied safe working conditions, particularly safer sex information in the language they understand.

Dorf hopes the Commission that she heads will one day be able to work with gay groups in developing countries to create a "responsible gay tourism mandate," the contents of which will be developed by those groups. "As a community, we need to have a responsible approach to tourism all over the world."

RETURN TO THE MALL

As the welts on the reddened butt cheeks of famed vandal Michael Fay fade in the collective memories of the American people, Singapore becomes another supervalue vacation—a tropical locale with a rum concoction named for it. But on the eighteen-hour flight to this place that I once called home, I feel an extraordinary sense of nostalgia, and a wedge of apprehension; there is blood in my memories.

Just my luck that I should be stuck in the same section of the airplane with thirty White Hindus—half of whom did not preorder the vegetarian meal—en route to Calcutta for a "Oneness Earth Peace Run." Why one of the youths had a tennis racquet with him is beyond my comprehension. The *coup de grace* of this whole experience was watching thirty White Hindus watching *True Lies*, Arnold Schwarzenegger's latest ultraviolent, penis-waving act of machismo.

It's strange that I consider Singapore home, since I'm not a citizen. However, by a sheer stroke of parentage, my mom's Singaporean, and I was afforded the benefits of the British education system with a twist of Singaporean ideology. Having spent twelve years living and studying and growing up there, I very much consider Singapore my home.

For the uninitiated, Singapore is a tiny island on the tip of the Malayan peninsula. It has absolutely no natural resources, so it lives on tourism, and has a reputation as a shrewd business hub; it has the busiest harbor and airport in the industrialized world. About three million people are crammed onto 244 square miles of land. This little island-state-republic has often been described as having a socialist government with a capitalistic economy and democratic elections. The same ruling party has run the country since it gained independence from Malaysia in 1965.

Singapore is a strange place. It is famed for its ban on chewing gum. On arrival at the port of call, travelers are warned of the consequences of not disposing of the chewing gum in their possession: a hefty fine. Apparently, the government felt they could save a massive cleanup bill if the city cleaners didn't have to scrape those nasty bits of chewed-up-and-spat-out sticky bits off buses, sidewalks, and other surfaces. All I can say is that it is nice to put your hands underneath a table, bench, or chair and not have to recoil in disgust when you accidentally touch one of those hardened lumps of cud.

There are others peculiarities, though.

I grew up with: the courtesy campaign, designed with a fluffy lion mascot instructing us how to be polite, reminding us to say "Thank You" and "Please"; the Speak Mandarin Only and Not Other Dialects campaign; the energy-saving campaign (I won second prize in the National Energy-Saving Quiz—Primary School

Division). There was the antispitting campaign. Again, hefty fines were levied. We were instructed to spit into a tissue and to discard the tissue into a waste receptacle. There was the skateboard ban. There was the anti–Killer Litter campaign: People who lived in high-rise flats would toss all forms of trash, kitchen and electrical appliances out of their windows, killing unfortunate and unsuspecting folk.

Then there were the Urine Detectors. These little gizmos were installed in elevators. If someone were to whiz in the elevator, as was often the case, the Urine Detector would kick into gear, stopping the elevator and starting the video camera overhead that would record the deed as evidence when the unfortunate person was finally charged in court and had his or her face splashed across the newspapers. The bastard sibling to the Urine Detector was the Toilet Flushing Device. This gizmo would ensure that the lock on the public toilet cubicle door would not reopen if you did not flush. Instead, alarms would be set off and a hefty fine awaited you.

And then there were the national songs. "Stand Up for Singapore," "Count on Me, Singapore," "The Productivity Song." Christ, were they catchy. They were played all over the telly, we were taught to sing them in school, and little kids would be humming them on the streets.

Peculiarities, perhaps, but when you grow up in such an environment and when such peculiarities are taken in all seriousness, earnestness, and with governmental enforcement, it all becomes something quite sinister indeed.

But here I am, coming home to a place that has lived through decades of this and has undoubtedly been scarred by the trade-off of freedoms for the promises of peace, prosperity, and progress. Yippee.

The Singapore where I grew up, came out, and left had changed considerably. It's busier, there are more people, CNN is everywhere, there are more malls, more shopping centers, more multiplexes, more technology. Everything seems to be a little neater, more ordered, and a lot more crowded.

The first place that I had to revisit was Plaza Singapura, an older shopping center, one of the first big ones, that housed the Japanese-owned megasupermarket Yaohan. Plaza Singapura has the reputation as being one of the cruisiest places in the country. It is certainly an institution of gay life in Singapore. Somehow, gay tourists, newly coming-out locals, and experienced sluts all manage to discover this place. Plaza Singapura holds a special place in my psyche. It is the place where I spent a considerable amount of time as a teenager having sex in the rest rooms and meeting men in the corridors.

Not much has changed. Lots of teenagers and men of all ages wander around looking nonchalant but still keeping a firm eye on the route to the bathroom. They hang around the atrium, at the escalators, and in the fire escapes waiting for, at the very least, a brief moment of homosexual passion.

I strike up a conversation with a young man named Tony. He's on his lunch break and looking for some action. Where does a gay person go to meet others? I ask. He doesn't know. This seems to be the only way he knows of in the whole damn country. He lists a few parks and malls where such meetings are reputed to happen. He wants to meet someone he can settle down with, but he doesn't seem to have any luck, he says.

An expatriate approaches me. He has left his boyfriend in a store shopping, he wants to try to set up a meeting later if possible, can he have my phone number? I politely decline his offer of a possible tryst.

In a bathroom, I meet a large West Indian man. He is happily rinsing off his cock in the sink. He shakes his dick at me, laughs, and says, "I just fucked a nice piece of ass. You Singapore boys are all so sex-crazy."

Things haven't changed so much.

Shopping malls and shopping centers are very much a defining part of Singapore. There are shopping centers everywhere, of varying sizes, catering to varying class levels.

Hanging out at malls is a large part of Singaporean life and the major pastime of many young people seems to be hanging out at malls. There is a very vibrant theater and arts scene, but damn, those malls always win out. But since the retail numbers are down, it figures that no one is really buying anything, they're just hanging out. This is, of course, not new. In the eighties, the mallies were called Centrepoint Kids, named after a then-new-and-hopping shopping center. It's a sign of the times: In neighboring Malaysia, the same effect is happening, though there, the syndrome is called Boh Sia or Lepak. Literally meaning "loitering," the implicit meaning is that these youths are directionless and un-motivated. It's the Southeast Asian version of the Generation-X malady that the American media bemoans.

But what else is there to do? Perhaps another interesting phe-nomenon is the boom in local writers of ghost and supernatural stories. The other current obsessions are starting a band, laser karaoke, arguing about what constitutes Asian values, and modeling. Ex-model Bonnie Hick's memoirs *Pardon Me, But Are You a Model* was a massive best-seller.

New to the Singapore experience is Sell-A-Vision, a late-night television program that is instantly recognizable as a local knock-off of the Home Shopping Network. And just what exactly is for sale? How about all the crap that never took off in America or the fads that died even before they happened. Chia pets are big; you can hardly leave the house and not be confronted by a stall hawking these little monsters. Also up for sale are stair-steppers, grilling machines, aromatherapy kits, slide aerobics kits, and the Thighmaster.

I'm bitten by the shopping-mall bug. I visit Raffles City. Raffles City consists of the Westin Plaza, two towering hotels built on top of a shopping center. The Westin is one of the tallest hotels in the world; on a clear day, you can just about see the coast of Indonesia from the top floor. Raffles City houses Sogo, a premiere Japanese department store. Apparently, Raffles City is fast becoming the new cruisy spot, stealing a lot of the thunder from Plaza Singapura.

There are the usual packs of cruisers: Another expatriate invites me to his house; a Kiwi tourist tells me about a shopping center in Los Angeles where the entire paneling comes off between toilet stalls. A local guy tells me he's in a long-distance relationship with a man in Belgium; he sees his lover once a year at best. This is not an uncommon situation.

Down the street from Raffles City is the Marina. Again, this is three hotels built around a large shopping center. When it was first built, there was a small Zen stream that flowed throughout the mall. Now that little stream is covered by makeshift stalls selling toys and electronics. Again, more cruising occurs. And by this time, it does get a little bit trying.

Back in the good old days, there were a slew of gay hangouts. There was the Lambda Bar, Niche, Legends, and Rumours, all of which were, not surprisingly, located in shopping centers. The Lambda Bar in Far East Shopping Center, Niche in Far East Plaza, Legends in Lucky Plaza, and Rumours in Wisma Atria. When AIDS came around, those bars and discotheques were closed down in the late eighties.

Now, there are plenty of clubs and discos around that gays and lesbians favor, though none that are as blatantly open about its clientele as they were in the heady eighties. None except for Vincent's.

Vincent's is like a depressing colonial version of Cheers. The bar is located on the fifth floor of Lucky Plaza in the heart of the tourist district. It is a very tiny, poorly lit place, with sliding doors. The wall by the entrance is decorated with cards from well-wishers on their travels around the world; farther in, there are small ink drawings of suggestive natural renderings: bulbous rocks and protruding sandstone phenomena.

Clutching my Tiger beer (later, I'll switch to tequila and OJ) on a Friday night, I watch the place slowly fill up with a motley assortment of tourists, locals, and expatriates. The place gets terribly smoky, and soon it is so cramped that there is hardly anyplace to move and the crowd spills over outside the doors.

Every wrinkled ghost of a European, no matter how shriveled and pickled, and who would, in the harsher realm of American bar culture, be referred to as "a fucking troll," seems to have some adoring youth attached to him. Among the locals, though, there is a great contempt for locals who seek out the old P-K's—*pek-kwei*, white ghosts, for whatever reason. But still, there is and has always been those that will attach themselves to the Western tourists and expatriates, perhaps for financial gain, a means to leave the country, or some sense of prestige. It's hard to blame them, though. It's understandable to want to fuck around with someone who has no ties to the place, someone who will not likely know their friends or family, and someone who they believe knows more about really being gay. Here at Vincent's, decades of gay life in Singapore come to a standstill, it is all at once, the past, the present, and the future.

An American expatriate is telling his chums about how work prospects are better in Singapore but the living is much better in Bangkok. Two drunk Australian tourists seem to get much attention from a small pack of giggling locals. An American is telling his local friends about how he's off to China for a tour. He's taking his class on a field trip to Tiananmen Square to fly kites, he says. A local guy invites me to go with his group to the nearby 7-Eleven to get more booze when the bar closes at 2 A.M. By 1 A.M. most of the pairing up has taken place. A lot of trade gets done in the rest room across the way.

I meet up with an old friend. In the days since, Gary has achieved some fame as an up-and-coming fashion designer, having represented the country in competitions in Japan and China.

Over the best bloody dim sum at the Goodwood Hotel, we reminisced about the good old days when we discoed our nights away to eighties aqua music. Aqua is the derogatory term for an effeminate gay person, and aqua music was the Communard's doing "Never Can Say Goodbye" and "Don't Leave Me This Way," Whitney Houston's "I Wanna Dance with Somebody," Baltimora's "Tarzanboy," Mel & Kim, Rick Astley, Sinitta, or any faceless Stock, Aitken, and Waterman–produced record, and everything by Bananarama. We reminisced about his fling with the engineer from Sydney and my fling with the Swedish psychologist. We compared photos of our current loves. Gary has been with his lover for three years now; they met while cruising at Plaza Singapura. He tells me that the porn magazines that I sent him years ago were the greatest, and they were passed around so much among his friends that he eventually lost track of all of them. He tells me an old flame of mine has become a very successful local playwright and is now in England pursuing a further degree. Things are still pretty much the same as they were six years ago when I left, Gary says, except there are fewer places to meet other homos. He's looking forward to coming to New York, he has won a scholarship to study there. "I just can't wait to leave, I'm so sick of this place," he says. I doubt if he's the only one. One of the government's concerns was that many young Singaporean girls were getting married to foreigners and expatriates and leaving the country. The argument goes that there are fewer women for Singaporean men. The government is big on procreation, especially between university graduates, and whatever the government wants, it makes sure it gets.

On the day I left, the *New Paper*—Singapore's afternoon tabloid which is something of a cross between *People*, the *Weekly World News*, and *New York Daily News*—runs their cover story: SINGA-PORE STRUGGLES WITH THORNY PROBLEM OF LESBIANISM, the headlines blare in forty-point type. It seems that many young girls are becoming lesbians.

Citing youth-counseling agencies and psychiatrists, the paper reports that there is a dire problem among fourteen- to eighteen-year-old girls. There are tomboys, who cut their hair short, bandage their chests, dress like boys, and have very feminine girl-friends. The feminine girlfriends, we learn, are "attractive and dressed trendily and wooed by their tomboyish 'boyfriends' with expensive presents, dinners, and outings to the disco."

The *New Paper* had previously run an exposé, complete with hidden camera pictures, about the perverts who hang out at pub-lic swimming pool locker rooms in order to watch men showering and changing their swim trunks.

There is something implicitly unsettling about leaving a homeland so thoroughly and returning to it later. I return like an archeolo-gist, digging among the ruins, looking for artifacts and trying to piece together an understanding of a part of my life that has been amputated. Phantom pains are a very real thing.

America is often spoken of as a nation of immigrants. There are many people new to this country, some will perhaps never see any-thing of their homelands again. The distance acquired triggers some sense to reclaim a sense of home and you spend a lot of time simply describing.

And, being fortunate enough to return, instead of finding everything I have held in my power of remembering and description, all I find is myself wandering like a zombie out of *Night of the Living Dead*, trapped in the shopping mall, looking for flesh.

A MANGY AFTERWORD

The writings in *Mongrel* span 1994 through 1997. I started life as a journalist. That was what I came to the United States to study. I started my stint in journalism at the University of Hawaii at Moana where I worked feverishly at the campus daily. I was sure that the daily rigorous life of a reporter was what I wanted, I was idealistic, hopeful. After a few years in Hawaii, I transferred to the journalism program at San Francisco State University. The program at San Francisco State showed me how much I did not want to be a journalist, and how much I did not have the temperament for it. The things that passed for a thought among some of my peers horrified me. Here, all these kids still honestly believed in pure objectivity, and this translated into not having an opinion. Many honestly believed that they were these empty vessels through which "news" passed through to the readers. Maybe my ego was crushed, too: A fellow student who managed to misspell her name on her résumé got higher grades than I did. I wanted to have my opinions, I wanted to be an activist, I wanted to do things that would change the world. Of course, I was much younger then, and so full of pep and vim.

I had not considered essay writing until 1994 when Robin Bernstein and Seth Silberman sent me a note asking me to contribute to the anthology they were editing of writings by queers born on or around Stonewall. I wasn't sure how to go about it but knew that I wanted to write something. Outside of my journalistic duties, I had also been writing poetry and fiction. I used the skills I acquired from those genres to write the essay, "Q-Punk Grammar." Soon, other offers to write essays, nonfiction, and more opinionated pieces came in.

Writing essays and opinion pieces are a strange thing for me. Growing up, I was the youngest in the family, and anytime I tried to participate in the family discussions at dinnertime, I was always derided and dismissed for being naive, ill-informed, and just plain wrong. I learned to not make my opinions known. I was always taught not to seek attention, not to argue, and not to challenge authority openly. So this collection of writings is a bit of a challenge for me; and admittedly, it is all making me terribly nervous and apprehensive. That this book might be read absolutely terrifies me. After all, essay writing is essentially an open invitation to readers to argue with me, and to challenge my thoughts and my opinions.

If anything, this work, for me, is also a political stand. As Asians, and as Asians in America, we are so often not encouraged to claim authority, to claim an opinion. There are historical reasons for this silence, and blood memory runs deep. With this book, I wanted to be able to do just that, claim authority even knowing full well that I may be wrong. It never seemed to stop anyone else, so why not me?

The wave of Asian family memoirs being churned out in the

United States, and abroad as well, attest to a fear of claiming authority. We are more comfortable writing biographically because then, any challenges made can be dismissed with "Ah! Who should know me and my family better than myself!" But Asians writing about their families is a rather subversive act as well, since we are so often taught to respect the family and never to speak of the family to strangers. Still, readers expect Asians to be filled with nothing but family stories, exotic little tales set in exotic little lands, and all ending with some great oriental lesson that is universally true.

The thing, too, about writing these pieces is that they are so tied to the time that they were written in. Not only do physical things change, for instance, some of the places in "Return to the Mall" no longer exist, but the other more intangible stuff changes, too. Political thoughts mature, social agendas change, situations evolve. My opinions and my outlook will also possibly change as I figure more things out. I would like to think that nothing in this book is definite, nothing set in stone, and that it is all subject to some change. And hopefully, a change for the better. I don't want to sound apologetic. Perhaps this is a book that will not age gracefully, but at least it will be one that entered into its time kicking.

NOTES

Whenever possible, only first names are used; otherwise, most of the names in these writings have been changed.

Slightly different versions of some of the writings in this book were previously published in various books and magazines:

"Monster" was published in *Q & A: Queer in Asian America* (Temple University Press), edited by David Eng and Alice Hom.

"Saved" was published in *The Progressive*. "Smile" was originally written for *The Progressive* as well, but they decided not to publish it. I thank the editors and board of the magazine for funding my travels and research to Southeast Asia.

"Q-Punk Grammar" was published in *Generation Q* (Alyson Press), edited by Seth Clark Silberman and Robin Bernstein.

"Currency" was published in *Queerly Classed* (South End Press), edited by Susan Raffo.

"The Endless Possibility of a Kiss in a Fevered Faraway Home" was published in the 1995 San Francisco Asian American Film Festival catalogue.

"The Crispy Edges of Pancakes" was published in *modern words.*

"Blah" and "Death of the Castro" were published in *On-Q Bay Area Magazine.*

"On Ass Tactics, Aztec Ticks, Aesthetics" was published in *p-form.*

"After Yoko" was published in "This Is Not Her," a limited edition artist book published by KiKi Gallery.

"Downloads" was an experimental video documentary conceived by Dan "Dewey" Schott and written and narrated by myself. The video consisted of a succession of images and still photos that were posted on newsgroups and web sites on the Internet, with a narration. Because we wanted to make the video as short and as immediate as possible, mirroring the immediacy and short attention span of cyberpornzits, we edited down the original script to about seven minutes. The script printed here is the original script for the project. The video has been seen at film festivals in San Francisco, New York, Mexico, and Amsterdam.

"Pardon Me, But Are You Mr. Asian?" was published on the *San Francisco Bay Guardian On-line* (www.sfbg.com).

"Return to the Mall" was published in *wilde.*

ACKNOWLEDGMENTS

The author wishes to thank all the editors of the books, magazines, anthologies, zines, and web sites where early versions of
these works first appeared. And for general goodness, the author
thanks Dave Thomson, Lisa Asagi, Lawrence Schimel, Mikel
Wadewitz, Zack Linmark, Jeffrey McDaniel, Decat, Dewey Schott,
Beth Lisick, Ames Adamson, and all the people who found themselves in these writings, whether they wanted to or not. For financial assistance during crucial times: the California Arts Council,
PEN American Center, PEN Center USA West.

ABOUT THE AUTHOR

Justin Chin was born in Malaysia and grew up in Singapore. He is the author of *Bite Hard* (Manic D Press), which was a finalist in the Firecracker Alternative Book Awards and the Lambda Literary Awards. His solo performances have been performed nationally. Chin has received fellowships and grants from the California Arts Council, the Djerassi Artist Residency, Franklin Furnace, PEN American Center, and PEN Center USA West. He was on the 1995 and 1996 San Francisco National Poetry Slam teams. He now lives in San Francisco.